JESUS CHRIST

IN EPHESIANS

JESUS CHRIST

IN EPHESIANS

A DEVOTIONAL COMMENTARY ON EPHESIANS

RON JAMES

THE UPPER ROOM
Nashville, Tennessee

Jesus Christ in Ephesians

Cover Design: Jim Bateman
Book Design: Thelma Whitworth
First Printing: January 1988 (10)
Library of Congress Catalog Card Number: 87-050704
ISBN: 0-8358-0569-7

Printed in the United States of America.

Dedication

In loving gratitude to Lois, wife and helpmate for more than thirty years, and to our four children, Steven, Kristen, Jennifer, and David, whose lives and whose love I value more deeply than I can ever say.

Contents

Introduction

One of my advantages in preparing this book for publication is that the task has forced me to live at depth in the book of Ephesians, to steep mind and heart in its contents. I have spent the better part of a year doing this, and as a result I feel tuned to the message and motivation of Paul as he writes so passionately to the believers in Ephesus. I have not lived as long or as intimately with another biblical book. Therefore I want nothing more than to help readers sense with me the soaring quality of the Ephesian letter, its lift and spirit, its light and intensity.

As the subtitle indicates, this is "A Devotional Commentary on Ephesians." Its writing is meant as encouragement for Christians, as inspiration for mind and heart, as teaching for all who want to strengthen the foundations of their faith, as a call of discipleship for all who want to follow Jesus, as a tool for those called to preach and to teach others the Christian way, and as a resource to deepen appreciation for this New Testament letter. It is not my intention to deal with scholarly and academic matters of date and place of writing, literary structure, doctrinal formulas, or arguments about authorship. These and other subjects dealt with in historical and literary criticism are beyond the scope and purpose of this volume. This writing is not a verse by verse commentary, nor is it exhaustive in addressing the subject matter of Ephesians. What this book does is address the salient passages of Ephesians, the letter's notable and principal sections. As the table of contents reveals, the approach of the commentary is to move progressively through the chapters of Paul's letter, showing their inherent unity, especially as Paul's attention is unchangeably fixed on Jesus Christ, who is the luminous center and unfading focus of the letter to the Ephesians.

I

SENT BY GOD

1. *The Expression of God's Love*

1:1-8

To read the opening verses of Ephesians is to be struck immediately by the number of references to Jesus Christ. In the salutation of the letter, which is a single sentence, Paul speaks of him three times:

> Paul, an apostle of Christ Jesus by the will of God,
> To the saints who are also faithful in Christ Jesus:
> Grace to you and peace from God our Father and the Lord Jesus Christ.

Paul's consciousness is filled with the name, his attention fixed and held by the name, his thoughts and emotions centered on the name of Jesus. When he picks up his quill to write, the name seems to flow forth joyously, covering the page.

Having greeted the Ephesians in the name of Jesus in his brief salutation, Paul breaks into a spontaneous exclamation of praise: "Blessed be the God and Father of our Lord Jesus Christ, who has blessed us in Christ with every spiritual blessing." One does not have to be a student of literature or biblical studies to know immediately that Paul's whole being is full of some momentous discovery inseparable from the name and person of Jesus Christ. What is the secret hidden in the name of Jesus that has been revealed to him? What mystery does he know that has created such gladness of heart? As this chapter's title indicates, it is the discovery that Jesus is the expression of God's love. In human form, in flesh and blood, at a specific time and place in history and in our midst, God expressed divine love for the world in a man named Jesus, who, as the theologians have often said, is the human face of God. This understanding of God's action, God's self-disclosure, is the heart of Paul's message. In some unique way in the end undefinable, God was in Jesus as God has never been in another—so much so that Jesus is God's word spoken, God's will disclosed, God's salvation revealed, God's justice proclaimed, and God's glory manifested.

One can speculate about the extent to which consciousness of this idea permeates the life of churches today. Not long ago a questionnaire came to my desk through denominational channels. One query asked about the theological position of the local church membership: Liberal? Conservative? Social activist? Evangelical? A friend of mine who received the same questionnaire pondered this and wrote down, "Vague theism." That minister believes that if the average member of his congregation were asked to write a statement of religious belief the answer would be, "There's gotta be somebody up there somewhere." Could this be a creed worth considering? Think how all-embracing it is, how inclusive, how uncomplicated. Everyone could ascribe to it: Zoroastrian, Muslim, Buddhist, Krishna follower, Christian, Jew. "There's gotta be somebody up there somewhere."

A faith comprised of vague generalities is hardly a faith

at all. It has little power to grip the mind and heart, to engage our energies, or to enlist us in the worship and service of God. Giving up the essentials of Christian faith is surrendering the very center of that faith. For Paul the center of faith is God's disclosure of himself in Jesus Christ. In the first eight verses of Ephesians, in the style and emotional tone of the writing as well as the content, we can observe something of the person of Christ, the passion of Christ, and the primacy of Christ.

The Person of Christ

There had never been any doubt for Paul that God was personal. Genesis sees God as the Creator of the world, the One whose spirit forms man and woman from dust and chaos, raises them up from the abyss of nothingness, and breathes life into the lifeless clay. Every man and woman on the face of the earth lives and moves by the creative breath of God. This is the grand declaration of Genesis. Furthermore, as Genesis teaches us, God has created humankind with whom to fellowship. The first man and woman walk and talk with God in the perfect garden called Eden. There is communion; there is mutuality; there is interchange. After all, Adam and Eve are animated by the life-force of God, bearing God's image indelibly on mind and spirit.

As the Old Testament unfolds, it reveals a God who summons women and men to share a common purpose. God calls Abram to be father of a new people and empowers Sarah to have a son, though she is past childbearing years. God calls Moses to lead Israel out of Egyptian bondage into a new land of freedom. Deborah is called by God to be a judge and David to be a king. God calls Isaiah, Jeremiah, and Amos to speak heavenly truth to royal power and to champion the cause of the weak and the poor. God, who is personal, communicates divine self and will to persons. Paul is steeped in this belief. It is basic to everything he knows about God.

This is not quite so basic for us living in the twentieth century! We look out on a universe of such magnitude that we are stunned. Our telescopes penetrate a vast cosmos in which there are more stars and planets than there are grains of sand on our little world. And, turning from macrocosm to microcosm, our microscopes penetrate the atom, uncovering mysteries beyond our comprehension. Here are tiny universes that store up an awe-inspiring power and complexity. Here are subatomic particles that dance halfway between matter and energy, defying the conventional principles of our earlier understandings of physics. But whether we look out a thousand light years into space or look into the mysterious heart of the atom, there is no God to be seen. Grand and wondrous forces in the physical world, yes! An upward movement from chaos to order in our planet, yes! Constant laws throughout the universe, sometimes defying description, yes! But no force we can identify, no principle we can isolate, no reality we can perceive that appears in any sense personal. At least not when we try to put God on the block for examination. No objective search, no scientific inquiry, no rational set of propositions will cause God to materialize before our eyes. We can neither prove nor disprove God; and while there is evidence enough to argue God's existence, there is never so much that we are spared the risk and adventure of faith.

Whatever difficulties many people in the twentieth century may have with a God who is personal, it is not so with Paul, and it is not so in the Bible. Neither Old

Testament nor New Testament are concerned with belief about God, but with trust in God. They keep on telling us that we can meet and know God and be rightly related to God. What God? Not an abstract "prime mover," in Aristotle's phrase, a first cause; not a faceless, formless, universal force; not natural law or evolution; but, for Paul, "the God and Father of our Lord Jesus Christ" (1:3). This is the glowing center for Christian Faith, the critical mass out of which the energy of Christianity rises. God, who is personal, is revealed in a person, Jesus, whom we call "the Christ." It follows that Christianity and Jesus himself remain opaque for us—impenetrable, obscure, remote, locked away in a holy book, until we, as persons, meet the God who is revealed in the person of Jesus Christ. Faith does not come when we try to decide *about* God, but when we submit ourselves *to* God, especially as we know God in Jesus. To such an experience, Dr. John A. Mackay bears witness in a book called *God's Order*:

> I was a lad of only fourteen years of age when, in the pages of the Ephesian Letter, I saw a new world. I found a world there which had features similar to a world that had been formed within me. After a period of anguished yearning, during which I prayed to God each night the simple words "Lord help me," something happened. After passionately desiring that I might cross the frontier into a new order of life which I had read about, which I had seen in others whom I admired, I was admitted in an inexplicable way, but to my unutterable joy, into a new dimension of existence. What had happened to me? Everything was new. Someone had come to my soul. I had a new outlook, new experiences, new attitudes to other people. I loved God. Jesus Christ became the center of everything.[1]

This experience of a living Christ present for us and within us carries the church across the generations.

The Passion of Christ

The style, emotional tone, and content of Ephesians 1:1-8 tell us something about the passion of Christ. One does not need to read further than these first few verses to realize that Paul is not a sociologist commenting on the cultural differences between Greeks, Jews, and Romans. He is also not a philosopher who goes about asking, "What is truth?" To call Paul a religious teacher does not capture the essence of his motivation or the inner force of his call. Above and beyond everything else he is an evangelist, a man captivated by a message. He sees himself as an ambassador to his world entrusted with the great secret of the gospel, the messenger of the mystery that God is in Christ "reconciling the world to himself" (2 Cor. 5:19). This mystery finds expression in the man Jesus of Nazareth, who is the unique servant and Son of God, crucified, dead, buried, but crowned by God with life and power in the resurrection. This risen Christ has stood full in Paul's path, confronted him, changed him, and commissioned him to tell Christ's name everywhere. It is for this name and cause that Paul is an evangelist. The person of Christ, met on the Damascus Road, has become the passion of Paul's life.

The opening of this chapter makes the point that the opening verses of Paul's letter are preoccupied with Jesus. His name is used six times, five pronouns refer to him, and Paul ascribes to him the Messianic title, "the Beloved One." Built into the letter the way steel girders are built into a high rise, Jesus Christ gives Ephesians its shape and strength and is the passion of Paul's writing.

If the New Testament letters are foundational for the church in every generation, it follows that Jesus, as he is revealed to us in the gracious will of a loving God, is to be the continuing center of the church's life. German theologian Jurgen Moltmann knows this when he writes, "Christian faith basically lives only as a profession of faith in Jesus."[2] In the Gifford Lectures, given by A.E. Taylor at the University of St. Andrew in Scotland between the years of 1926 and 1928, one reads similar sentiments: "If we ask ourselves seriously what it is in Christianity which is the element of supreme value to Christians . . . what it is *they* find in Christianity and nowhere else, I do not think there can be any doubt about the answer; it is . . . the person of Christ himself, taken as the completest revelation of God."[3]

The Apostles' Creed is the earliest of the church's creeds, finding its roots in early baptismal questions in the second and third centuries. It is a statement of Christian essentials representing the faith of the early church. Of its 110 words, 70 refer directly to Jesus. The passion of this creed is Christ.

The Primacy of Christ

Simply put, Paul's point of view would be that because of Jesus of Nazareth's life, death, and resurrection, through which he is revealed as the Christ, the church is born. Jesus himself, in the midst of the Easter daybreak, commissions the church to "make disciples of all nations" (Matt. 28:19). It is not the church which gives birth to Jesus, but Jesus who gives birth to the church. He is primary. To put it one way, the church is the lengthened shadow of its founder. It exists to bear witness to his name, loving and serving the world for his sake.

I can remember joking that after his conversion, when Paul went up to Jerusalem to confer with the apostles, he was met by a committee. Nothing can be accomplished without organization. Jesus had said, "You shall be my witnesses in Jerusalem and in all Judea and Samaria and to the end of the earth" (Acts 1:8). Here is a calling and a task that will require institutional structures: strategy and planning, councils and committees, boards and agencies, preachers and teachers, fund-raising. The apostles would not be able to respond to Jesus' command without an institution. It becomes the vehicle to carry the message of Christ.

Writing about the established church at the beginning of the Protestant Reformation, Jaroslav Pelikan says, "Captive in ecclesiastical structures that no longer served as channels of divine life and means of divine grace, the spiritual power of the Christian gospel pressed to be released."[4] Those of us who have been members in churches or leaders in churches realize that, like all human institutions, the church is imperfect. Sometimes it is weak; often it is blind to its own faults; its leaders, lay and clergy alike, have feet of clay. When we read the history of the church's journey across the years, flawed as that history is, we are convinced that only by the grace of God has the message of the gospel reached the twentieth century. It is true both for the individual Christian and the institutional church. As Paul said in Second Corinthians 4:7, "We have this treasure in earthen vessels, to show that the transcendent power belongs to God and not to us." The conclusion we must reach, while not profound, is critically important for the vitality of the church: Jesus is primary! He does not exist for the sake of the institutional church like some kind of hallmark label;

it is the church which exists for the sake of Jesus, who is head of the church and Lord of the church. As such, he is the expression of God's love. To lose sight of that is to miss the meaning of it all.

Let me lift up Paul's definition of what it means to be a Christian: The Christian man or woman is one who is "in Christ." It is a formula Paul uses. One finds it ten times in Ephesians 1:3-14. The person "in Christ" is the person rightly related to God through an acceptance of Jesus' life, death, and resurrection. To put it another way, the Christian is one who finds God or is found by God through Christ. That person realizes that such is a gift beyond earning or deserving. Forgiveness and acceptance are present realities; resistance and rebellion are overcome in the warmth of the Christ who dwells within. Those who stand within this awareness know the meaning of Paul's salutation, "Grace to you and peace from God our Father and the Lord Jesus Christ" (Eph. 1:2). Whatever Christian church they happen to be in, whatever its organization, its imperfection, its combination of strength and weakness, they know that Jesus is primary.

In style and tone, as well as the content of these first eight verses of Ephesians 1, Paul presents Jesus Christ as the expression of God's love. Reflected in Paul's heart and mind we see something of the person of Christ, the passion of Christ, and the primacy of Christ, which will enable the church in any generation to live with integrity and power.

Notes

1. John A. Macay, *God's Order: The Ephesian Letter and This Present Time* (New York: The Macmillan Company, 1957), p. 6.
2. Jurgen Moltmann, *The Crucified God* (New York: Harper & Row, Publishers, 1974), p. 82.
3. A. E. Taylor, *The Faith of a Moralist*, Vol. II (New York: The Macmillan Company, 1930; New York: Kraus Reprint Corporation, 1969), p. 118.
4. Jaroslav Pelikan, *Spirit Versus Structure* (New York: Harper & Row, Publishers, 1968), p. 5.

2. *The Mystery of God's Will*

1:9-10

We love a mystery. Something within us wants to believe that our lives mean more than waking and sleeping, eating and drinking, getting and spending. Is this all there is? Is the meaning of the world exhausted in market reports? Can we reduce it all to mathematics, chemistry, and statistics? Do the physical sciences explain it all, robbing us of anything transcendent? Wordsworth must have been asking himself these questions when he wrote:

> The world is too much with us; late and soon,
> Getting and spending, we lay waste our powers:
> Little we see in Nature that is ours:
> We have given our hearts away.[1]

Yet there remains within us a persistent fascination with things we can neither explain nor understand. Perhaps we hope those things come to us from another dimension of reality. That's why we used to tune in "I Love a Mystery" and "Mystery Theater" on the radio. That's why television programs like "The Twilight Zone" had good ratings. That's why films like *Star Wars, Alien,* and

Close Encounters of the Third Kind made so much money. That's why, a generation or two ago, people read mystery writers H. Rider Haggard and Edgar Allen Poe's tales about the dark side of life. We love a mystery. We long for there to be a dimension of reality bigger than we are, for we sense a meaning—a depth to life beyond the things we can see and touch.

The Ephesian passage this chapter seeks to examine is a passage about mystery. These verses put the mind in a whirl. *Lofty* is scarcely the descriptive word for the passage, for it draws us into a transcendent realm, a future world in which God's kingdom has come and God's will is done in a united heaven and earth. Anyone who seeks to comment on these verses feels dwarfed by their majesty and inadequate to the task. Listen to the words: "He has made known to us in all wisdom and insight the mystery of his will, according to his purpose which he set forth in Christ as a plan for the fulness of time, to unite all things in him, things in heaven and things on earth."

A lot of us are "hands-on" people. We feel more comfortable if the things we do and the thoughts we think are concrete. For one reason or another, we grow uneasy when talk turns to airy things like mystery, intangible things like faith, or indefinable things like the presence of God. Yet, difficult as these things may be, they stretch our minds and surely tell us something essential about who we are and the kind of a universe in which we live. Maybe a passage from Loren Eiseley will open a door:

> While I was sitting one night with a poet friend watching a great opera performed in a tent under arc lights, the poet took my arm and pointed silently. Far up, blundering out of the night, a huge Cecropia moth swept past from light to light over the posturings of the actors.

> "He doesn't know," my friend whispered excitedly. "He's passing through an alien universe brightly lit but invisible to him. He's in another play; he doesn't see us. He doesn't know. Maybe it's happening now to us. Where are we? Whose is the *real* play?"[2]

Do you know that as you read these lines you are not still, as it seems, but, as Annie Dillard points out, "in orbit around the sun," you are "moving 64,800 miles an hour. The solar system as a whole, like a merry-go-round unhinged, spins, bobs, and blinks at the speed of 43,200 miles an hour along a course set east of Hercules"?[3]

Have you ever held an ancient fossil in your hand, watched a shooting star, or contemplated a mountain or a tiny flower without experiencing in a deep inner place "some dark suggestion that the things nearest to us stretch far beyond our own power, some sacramental feeling of the magic in material substance"?[4]

From what I have heard, the gold ring on your finger or the gold chain around your neck had its origin in an alien part of the universe. That is, an element as heavy as gold could not have been formed by our sun, since there is not enough heat at the core of the sun nor ever has been to form an element as heavy as gold. It was formed in a sun much larger than ours. There's a little mystery in that.

Why are we religious at the core of our being? Why this undeniable impulse to pray? Why is no civilization without an altar? In times of tragedy, danger, or despair, why do we instinctively cry out, "O God, help me"? Why have people always told and retold their experiences of God? Is this simply superstition or whistling in the dark, or is there a vast invisible reality that underlies our entire existence—a reality in which we "live and move and have our being" (Acts 17:28)? And, if so, are there not points at which that reality intersects our own? Better yet, are there not pieces of our own lives, our own human nature, that instinctively recognize what the New Testament calls "the kingdom of God"? Are there not unconscious impulses within us that seek God?

How important are these deep human questions in an age immersed in technological advance? How easy to be so absorbed by the dazzling material goodies technology makes available that we lose our capacity for wonder, our sensitivity to mystery. This is when the human spirit begins to suffocate. This text, therefore, has much to say to us: "[God] has made known to us . . . the mystery of his will." Let me provide some historical background. In Paul's day the conventional religions of Greece and Rome were as stale as yesterday's coffee. For one thing, nobody really believed in Zeus, Diana, or any of the gods and goddesses of the Roman pantheon. State-sponsored temple rites were boring. There were ritual prayers for the city-state, the tribe, the family, but little about the individual. The religion was dry as dust, formal, barren of emotion. That's why the mystery religions were flourishing. We do not know a lot about them, since the mysteries were jealously guarded. But we know some things. Mystery religions were in ascendence for several centuries, worshiping such deities as Isis and Osiris, Dionysus, and Mithra and Cybele. Highly emotional in their appeal, intensely personal, these religions promised salvation and immortality. And what, in fact, were the mysteries? Why were they so jealously guarded? They were the secret worship practices that were the divine knowledge of the cult and that guaranteed the presence of the divinity and the salvation of the worshiper. What kind of practices? Sacred story, secret rite, symbolic action, dance, drama, chant, and song. The destiny of the god or goddess was portrayed somewhat like a medieval mystery play, portrayed in such a way that the devotees felt themselves to share in the failure and triumph of the one whom they worshiped.

One must imagine the mood of such a worship experience: Torch light in an underground grotto, sacrifices dripping blood, robed priests in the mask of the gods, drums and dancing figures in the firelight, solemn warnings that if anything were revealed the persons breaking the trust would suffer the vengeance of the gods. Any who wish to participate in the mysteries must join with others in a long and involved period of initiation—many different offerings, purifications, sacred oaths and vows of fidelity. At last the time approaches when the final secret is whispered into the ear of the initiate by the high priest—in the torchlight, in the midst of the throbbing of the liturgy—so that the initiate now possesses the secret and the gods of the secret. The mystery has been revealed; salvation has come.

This had power in Paul's day! When he said, "God has made known to us the mystery of his will," just about everybody in that day heard the word *mystery* against the background of the mystery religions. Does this make Paul the spokesman of one more mystery religion and one more god, this one named Jesus Christ? Far from it, and here's why: First, Paul was a Jew, and, as a Jew, detested pagan religion. Nothing could have been more offensive to Paul than the so-called gods and goddesses of the mysteries. A Jew would die rather than worship a pagan image or accept a pagan ritual. Second, Paul's teaching about Jesus as the Christ can never be traced to pagan origins. It is abundantly clear that Jesus is unintelligible apart from Old Testament Judaism. The Law, the Prophets, the Messianic hope alone explain and interpret Jesus as the Christ. Third, Paul presents Jesus not as one among many, but as the unique and only Son of God.

Why then does Paul speak of Jesus as the mystery, the secret revealed by God? Not by way of comparison, but by way of contrast. To draw an analogy, someone who had been addicted to cocaine and had then become a follower of Jesus, breaking free from the drug habit, might say, "Hey! If you want to get high, get high on Jesus! It's a whole lot better and lasts a whole lot longer!" Even though that person says, "high," the experience of drugs and the experience of Jesus are not being compared but contrasted. The former addict is speaking a language drug addicts can understand. "If you want to get hooked, get hooked on Jesus!" Paul is a good communicator, so he says to people who were steeped in knowledge about the mystery religions, "If you want to know the divine secret, listen to this. If you want to meet and know God, listen to this. Jesus is the secret! He is God's mystery, hidden from the beginning of time, but now revealed. Step a little closer and let me tell you about it." Paul, a Jew, is speaking to a Gentile world in language Gentiles can understand.

Our text says that the mystery of God's will has been made known in Christ. If indeed it is a secret, it is an open secret, for God has uncovered the secret for all to see. Paul talks about this in several of his letters: "Jesus Christ . . . the revelation of the mystery which was kept secret for long ages but is now disclosed" (Rom. 16: 25-26); "the mystery of Christ, which was not made known . . . in other generations as it has now been revealed to his holy apostles and prophets by the Spirit" (Eph. 3:4-5); "God's mystery, . . . Christ, in whom are hid all the treasures of wisdom and knowledge" (Col.

2:2-3). These verses leave no doubt about the essence and content of the mystery revealed by God. It is Jesus as the Christ, who not only reveals the mystery but is himself the mystery. God has chosen to incarnate the mystery of the divine loving purpose in Jesus of Nazareth.

These verses also leave no doubt that the mystery is for the world. Though it springs from the soil of Judaism, it is universal in its message and is to be proclaimed among the Gentiles. Those to whom the secret is revealed and becomes real are charged with the task of making it known to others. The secret is that God loves the world, each of us and all of us in our ignorance, in our doubt and rejection, in our fear and mortality, in our failure and sin; loves us with the intention of winning our love and our allegiance, of calling us to a purpose broader than our own comfort and success. That secret does not come to us as a piece of information, not even a holy book or a creed, but in the giving of Jesus Christ. This is the secret now disclosed, that at the center of this mysterious cosmos is not unreasoning chance or blind force, but an infinite love in the full dimension of that word, whom the New Testament calls "the God and Father of our Lord Jesus Christ."

Much of the power of these two verses in Ephesians 1 lies in the cosmic dimension of the secret they address. The Jesus who bends his back beneath his cross on the way to Calvary, who drinks the bitter cup of humiliation and death for our sake is not the focus of attention. It is not the suffering servant whose "appearance was so marred, beyond human semblance" (Isa. 52:14), but a risen and ascended Christ with a face "like the sun shining in full strength" (Rev. 1:16). It is a Christ who, from the other side of death, says to his disciples, "All authority in heaven and on earth has been given to me" (Matt.

28:18). Madeleine L'Engle paints the picture well in a passage from *The Irrational Season*. She tells of visiting a church in Istanbul called "The Church of the Chora." It was a chill morning with the smell of the first snow in the air:

> As we stepped over the threshold we came face to face with a slightly more than life-size mosaic of the head of Christ, looking at us with a gaze of indescribable power. It was a fierce face, nothing weak about it, and I knew that if this man had turned such a look on me and told me to take up my bed and walk, I would not have dared not to obey. And whatever he told me to do, I would have been able to do.
>
> The mosaic was preparation for the fresco over the altar. I stood there, trembling with joy, as I looked at this magnificent painting of the harrowing of hell. In the center is the figure of Jesus striding through hell, a figure of immense virility and power. With one strong hand he is grasping Adam, with the other, Eve, and wresting them out of the power of hell. The gates to hell, which he has trampled down and destroyed forever, are in cross-form, the same cross on which he died.[5]

"A plan for the fulness of time," says the text, a time when "all things . . . in heaven and things on earth" will be united in Christ. What does that mean? We really don't know in any kind of concrete and specific way. We use words like *eschatology*. We talk about the consummation of the age or the coming of the kingdom of God in its fullness, but we are unable to furnish details of that great "day of the Lord." It is, of course, the horizon of our faith and plays a central part in what we call "the Christian hope." There is a sense in which this world is prelude and then the symphony begins, though we dare not use that belief to denigrate this life or to escape from its joys and responsibilities. We embrace life here with its pain and promise, and we see it against the horizon of that which is to come. Mystery. The time when all things are united in Christ is just that—a mystery. We seek to make it no less, nor can we. We trust the future because we trust in Christ, who is the key to the mystery and through whom God's kingdom comes and God's will is done.

Notes

1. William Wordsworth, "The World Is Too Much with Us: Late and Soon," in *The Complete Poetical Works of William Wordsworth* (New York: Thomas Y. Crowell & Co.), p. 398.
2. Loren Eiseley, *The Unexpected Universe* (New York: Harcourt, Brace & World, Inc., 1969), pp. 175-76.
3. Annie Dillard, *Pilgrim at Tinker Creek* (New York: Harper Magazine Press, 1974; New York: Bantam Books, Inc., 1975), p. 23.
4. Gilbert K. Chesterton, *The Everlasting Man* (New York: Doubleday & Company, 1955), p. 108.
5. Madeleine L'Engle, *The Irrational Season* (Minneapolis: Seabury Press, 1977), p. 95.

3. *The Cosmic Scope of God's Purpose*
1:10-14

Let me tell you about this word *cosmic*. To say the least, it's a big word. Anyone who reads a major news magazine or has even a passing interest in astronomy knows that the cosmos is the universe out there. They tell us it is infinite in dimension. The statistics that people are always citing numb the mind. In discussing how galaxies explode, Paul W. Hodge gives us an idea of the power in these explosions:

> Consider a solar system, a star with one million planets, each with a million countries, each with a million cities, each with a million buildings, each with a million rooms, each with a million atomic bombs. And then imagine what would happen if you set off the bombs in this planetary system. You would have the size of explosion that we find when we look at a galaxy in explosion.[1]

As Mortimer Adler observes, there is "well-established evidence that the universe is constantly expanding, the galaxies moving apart at increasing velocity. . . . Somewhere between fifteen and twenty billion years ago, the world began with an explosion of cosmic dimensions."[2]

When you have said "cosmic," you have said more than "big"; you have also said "mysterious." Many scientists think the present cosmos originated from a lump of matter no bigger than an apple in a "big bang" that began all things and is still visible in an expanding universe. But the mystery is not exhausted in the sheer size of the universe, nor in its numberless stars and planets. Vast as it is, the cosmos seems to be an interconnected whole, a single web of reality with uniform laws, a seamless robe. Physicists have become the new mystics, saying that the universe is composed of "mind-stuff," that there are no clear distinctions between the Natural and the Supernatural, that "there is a higher power, not influenced by our wishes, which finally decides and judges."[3]

Cosmos is a Greek word. Originally it meant "to place in order," like setting a table or drawing a company of soldiers into ranks. It also meant "to adorn," and from it we get our word *cosmetic*. When we get up in the morning and see the image staring back at us from the glass, we know it is important to get our face in order.

As ancient Greeks observed the movement of the stars and planets, they began to apply the word *cosmos* to the sky. They meant, "The order by which the sum of individual things is gathered into a totality." As they observed the face of the night sky, they saw that all moved in a precise order. The heavenly bodies were not random or haphazard in their journeys. For Plato, everything in the cosmos, each object and creature, heaven and earth, god and person are brought together into one by universal order.[4] *Cosmos* became one of the most important and unique terms in Greek thought.

In view of all this, let us examine the scripture passage around which this chapter is built, Ephesians 1:10-14. Although the last chapter was built around verses 9 and

10, these verses are an inseparable part of our explorations in this chapter: "For [God] has made known to us . . . the mystery of his will, according to his purpose which he set forth in Christ as a plan for the fulness of time, to unite all things in him, things in heaven and things on earth." This sentence is the key sentence in Ephesians. Like the Greek concept of *cosmos,* it sets a vision for the fundamental order of all things. For Greek philosophers and twentieth-century physicists alike, it has a feeling for unity, for the mystical cord that binds all things together, the law to which all creation gives assent. It is God's purpose and plan, says the passage, that one day, in the fullness of time, God will bring all things together in Christ. The whole cosmos moves toward a culmination, a final harmony. This is basic to what Christians believe.

But that day is not yet. In fact, one need only open the daily paper to find and feel the very opposite: Chaos! It doesn't matter what day you choose; there will be stories about murder, robbery, child abuse, seething international hatreds that keep breaking out in violence, poverty, hunger, prejudice. To check the daily witness to chaos, I opened my local paper on a particular day and found that near Guadalajara, Mexico, two decomposed bodies had been unearthed that the authorities were almost certain were the bodies of a kidnapped American drug enforcement agent and a Mexican pilot. The site of the grim discovery was a ranch where there had been a recent shootout between Mexican police and suspected drug dealers. A second item in the same paper reported that forensic scientists in Toronto were trying to determine whether a scalp found in a car driven by an accused cop killer belonged to the car's owner, a woman from Mount Vernon, New York, who had disappeared several days earlier. A third item informed readers that about one out of three people using emergency shelters in Connecticut is probably mentally ill.

In addition to all of this is an ominous gray backdrop: the threat of nuclear war. The United States, Russia, and the rest of the world continue to look down the barrel of larger and ever larger nuclear cannons. We have the capability, so they tell us, to destroy the human race and with it this indescribably beautiful planet and its delicately balanced systems of life. What dark and dreadful force drives us to such a time of terror? It is as if some mysterious kingdom of death struggles against life and light. No wonder the poet wrote:

> I, a stranger and afraid
> In a world I never made.[5]

It does not take a theologian to conclude that the chaos "out there" in the world begins "in here" in the individual human heart. At a very basic level, we are at war with ourselves, divided within, confronted by a dark side of our own human nature that would waste our substance by obscuring the face of God and neighbor. A classic passage that describes this inner turmoil is Romans 7:19, 21: "I do not do the good I want, but the evil I do not want is what I do. . . . So I find it to be a law that when I want to do right, evil lies close at hand."

We are not what we ought to be, are we? We do not live up to the best that is in us. We fail repeatedly to walk in light and live in love. That's why counsellors and therapists are so busy. That's why the church advocates and practices confession. That's why guilt lives in us all. That's why the world is in such a mess. What are we talking about? You and me, our disunity, our lack of harmony, our confusion, our destructive behavior, and all the pain and sorrow that go with it. The world outside and the world inside are marked by division and chaos. To make this point about the dark side of life is not to concentrate on negatives but simply to bear witness to human experience. It is a way to address what we commonly call "the problem of evil." Notice this, therefore: The New Testament only speaks about cosmos against the dark background of chaos. As a matter of fact, the whole of Christianity is addressed to this profound darkness, to what the Bible would call "sin and death." The reach of Christianity, its grandeur and drama, its universal scope become visible only when we recognize the pervasive power of the chaos which holds the world in bondage.

And what is God doing about all of this? It is God's mysterious purpose, says the text, to set forth a plan for the fullness of time. What plan? To unite all things in Christ! It is a plan to restore the lost order—a plan to resolve everything that is discordant into a final harmony in which "they shall not hurt or destroy in all my holy mountain; for the earth shall be full of the knowledge of the Lord as the waters cover the sea" (Isa. 11:9). How will God bring it to pass? The New Testament witness is this: In Christ, who bears the very stamp of God's nature, God will strike evil at its root. God will smite the monster of chaos, destroying death itself. This is what cross and resurrection are all about and why they are front and center on the New Testament stage. The Easter hymn puts it well:

> The powers of death have done their worst,
> But Christ their legions hath dispersed:
> Let shouts of holy joy outburst. Alleluia![6]

Every time Jesus healed someone who was ill, every time he broke the grip of chaotic evil in someone's life, every time his gracious presence set somebody free from one kind of bondage or another, it was a sign of God's liberating order. The biblical phrase that stands as symbol for that order is "the kingdom of God." It means "the rule of God," God's sovereign dominion. That is why Jesus chose one shining sentence to crystallize his mission: "The kingdom of God is at hand; repent, and believe in the gospel" (Mark 1:15). What was promised ages ago in the experience of Israel and through the writers of the scripture is now ready for fulfillment. The presence and power of that kingdom are in Jesus. When evil has done its worst, when betrayal, condemnation, scourging, crucifixion, and death are past, God renders a judgment against chaos by raising Jesus from death. Peter's Pentecost preaching is powerful when he says, "God raised him up, having loosed the pangs of death, because it was not possible for him to be held by it" (Acts 2:24).

Every time a church adorns its steeple with a cross or sets one in the center of the sanctuary, it bears witness that Jesus is the emissary of a new age. Every time Christians spread their fragrant lilies across the chancel on an Easter morning, they declare their allegiance to a kingdom in which life and not death is the great reality. It is a belief anchored in experience, an in-the-bones awareness that "the old has passed away, behold, the new has come" (2 Cor. 5:17). Those of us who call ourselves by Christ's name declare ourselves against the reign of chaos and for the reign of God's order with its granite pillars of faith, hope, and love.

In verse 10, the text says that God's plan for the fullness of time is to unite all things in Christ. Let me try to track that truth a different way by appealing to human experience. As a matter of fact, this is just what the text does. After stating its broad theme of the final unity of all things in Christ, it appeals to the experience of the reader: "In him [Christ] you also, who have heard the word of truth, the gospel of your salvation, and have believed in him, were sealed with the promised Holy Spirit, which is the guarantee of our inheritance until we acquire possession of it, to the praise of his glory."

That which God purposes for the whole creation, that final harmony toward which the whole creation moves is anchored in the experience of the individual Christian. It is as if the one who believes, becoming part of the plan, moves into a field of force. When one has said yes to God's purposes in Christ, a resident energy accompanies that commitment. There is inner confirmation and sense of rightness. It is, as verse 14 says, a "guarantee of our inheritance." The Greek word for guarantee means "down payment" or "earnest money." The Holy Spirit confirms in our experience the kingdom that will one day come in its fullness.

Surely there is a universal human hunger for unity. We crave closeness to others, and moments of harmony and understanding between people are peak moments of happiness. At the center of worship and at the heart of prayer is our desire for unity with God. We feel completed in the mutuality of loving acceptance. Teilhard de Chardin, in some paragraphs on "Love as Energy," asks, "How can we account for that irresistible instinct in our hearts which leads us towards unity . . . ?"[7] To use an old analogy, as the spokes of a wheel come closer together in coming closer to the hub, so we humans come closer together in coming closer to God. The world may be full of chaos, but our basic longing is for unity. It is a fundamental inner reality, this dream of a golden age, when

> The wolf and the lamb shall feed together,
> the lion shall eat straw like the ox; [and]
> They shall not hurt or destroy in all
> my holy mountain, says the Lord.
>
> —Isaiah 65:25

We must move toward a final idea or perhaps fill out an idea already begun. The Christ who fills the consciousness of the New Testament writers, who is the soul of the gospels and letters, is no simple wayside prophet of another day. This is the Christ in whom all the purposes of God culminate. He is the Christ of Revelation who is Alpha and Omega, the beginning and the end, who says, "All authority in heaven and on earth has been given to me" (Matt. 28:18). It is the awesome Christ of Easter whom death cannot hold captive and who stands triumphantly in the light of the eternal morning. It is the Christ of First Corinthians, of whom Paul says: "Then comes the end, when he delivers the kingdom to God the Father after destroying every rule and every authority and power. For he must reign until he has put all his enemies under his feet. The last enemy to be destroyed is death. 'For God has put all things in subjection under his feet' " (15:24-27).

Our Ephesians text says that it is God's purpose "to unite all things to him [Christ], things in heaven and things on earth." What is God's plan? To resolve all discord into a final harmony, to unite all broken lines in Christ, to overcome everything that separates us from God's love and from one another, breaking the power of death over our world in all of its forms.

Yes, I know we see through a glass darkly, and I know there is much mystery here. I know our world is so battered and divided that our human eyes can see no resolution. But one thing we do see is Jesus. Because he is bringing order to our own lives, the Spirit confirms in us the beginnings of the final triumph of the reign of God. This is where we cast our anchor and commit our lives.

Notes

1. Paul W. Hodge, *The Revolution in Astronomy* (New York: Holiday House, 1970), p. 50.
2. Mortimer Adler, *How to Think about God* (New York: The Macmillan Company, 1980), p. 32.
3. Annie Dillard, pp. 207-8.
4. *Theological Dictionary of the New Testament*, vol. 3 (Grand Rapids, MI: Wm. B. Eerdmans Publishing Co., 1965), p. 871.
5. Alfred Edward Houseman, XII "Last Poems," in *The Collected Poems of A.E. Houseman* (New York: Holt, Rinehart and Winston, 1965), p. 111.
6. "The Strife Is O'er," trans. Francis Pott, in *The Hymnal*, vol. 2 (Presbyterian Board of Christian Education, 1933), no. 164.
7. Pierre Teilhard de Chardin, *The Phenomenon of Man* (New York: Harper & Row, Publishers, 1965), p. 266.

4. The Revelation of God's Power

1:15-23

Power is a luminescent word. Like a central star, its gravitational pull is almost irresistible. And like a star, its warming energy can bring life or can wither and blast with its strength until no life is possible. That's why *power* is also an ambiguous word, for we cannot look at the world around us without being fascinated by the many ways power is used. What good it can accomplish and what havoc it can cause, depending on the disposition of those who hold and use power.

It would be hard, for instance, to deny that international politics has always been a power game. "Might makes right" is the old saying. Beneath whatever words are said or whatever lofty principles are spoken, there is the reality of material might and military force. Abraham Heschel is right when he says, "History is first of all what man does with power."[1]

On the personal level, how natural for us to want to gather and use power to shape our own lives; power in whatever form—money, influence, position, physical strength, skill, intelligence, experience, information. And how easy for us to misuse power in controlling the destiny of others for our own benefit. Where do you draw the line? Surely it is right to seek our own security. But when does this curtail the freedom and security of those around us? When does a hunger to secure our own wealth or position obscure the needs of others? How do we treat people in the places where we have power: family, work, church, social club, civic or political committee?

We talk about power a lot in American culture. There is muscle power, horsepower, atomic power, purchasing power, and power over others. There is political power, military power, industrial power, and the power of the press. We talk about having clout and using clout, and no one wants to be considered weak or powerless. Surely the American preoccupation with violence betrays a power obsession that permeates American consciousness. It is so overwhelming that one scarcely knows where to begin. For one thing, the media inundates the public with reports of violence. Why do we want to hear it and see it? Why do they spell it out in such detail? Playwright Arthur Miller wrote after the murder of Robert Kennedy, "There is violence because we have daily honored violence. Any half-educated man in a good suit can make his fortune by concocting a television show whose brutality is photographed in sufficiently monstrous detail."[2] Whatever the historical and cultural reasons for it, it is hard to escape the judgment that we have become voyeurs of violence.

The passage in Ephesians upon which this chapter seeks to comment is a passage about the nature of God's power. The focus of the passage is found in the title of this chapter, which declares that Jesus Christ is "The Revelation of God's Power."

Paul's Prayer for Enlightenment

The passionate appeal of Paul's language is hard to miss. No academic lecture this, no theological treatise, no moral admonition. Here is a man who writes out of an enraptured heart, bearing good news out of his own rich spiritual experience. The man and the message are one. Listen to him speak: "You Ephesians, how I thank God for you! I want you to know that I am praying for you! And this is my prayer: That the darkness may roll back before the illumination God sends you. This all-glorious Father will give you the spirit of wisdom, so that within your own deepest self you will see and know God through Jesus Christ" (AP). These words are spoken by one whose own darkness has been rolled back in the Damascus Road vision of a living Christ. Paul is now agent of the same illuminating vision and the transforming changes it brings. He is as filled with this revelation as a room is filled with light. It is as if he says, "Hear what I am hearing, see what I am seeing, feel what I am feeling by making yourselves open to the way God is making himself known in Jesus Christ."

How do we do that? Not necessarily by taking Religion 101 at the university, by making a list of rational proofs for God's existence, or by trying to live a moral life, as good as these things might be. Neither separately nor together will they guarantee spiritual enlightenment, for only a passionate search from the heart brings illumination. The doors of spiritual perception do not open until one's very being is engaged in the quest for God. That is what made the psalmist cry out,

> As a hart longs
>   for flowing streams,

so longs my soul
  for thee, O God,
My soul thirsts for God,
  for the living God.
—42:1-2

If there are a lot of Americans who admit no such hunger, and there are, it may be that this materialistic age has clouded their spiritual and intuitive faculties until they do not ask the great human questions every generation has asked: Who am I? What is the meaning of my life? Where is truth? How can I know God? Perhaps a technological civilization such as ours is so absorbed in tangible realities that it loses touch with such intangible and unpragmatic realities as faith, hope, and love. It might behoove us every once in a while to remember that even Neanderthal man buried his dead with offerings.

Paul's appeal to the Ephesians for openness to spiritual enlightenment is relevant for us. Listen to Paul's phrases, "I am praying for you . . . that the darkness may roll back . . . the illumination God himself sends you. This all-glorious Father will give you the spirit of wisdom so that within your deepest self you will see and know God through Jesus Christ." The primary importance Paul places on spiritual enlightenment speaks forcibly to our day. What importance do we place on spiritual illumination, on the nurture and growth of the inner life, on the quest for God? Why are so many people impatient with this language? Hey! Let's go down to the really important matters: How is the Dow-Jones industrial average doing? What's on television tonight?

The temptation is to consign all these vague ideas about inner light to a compartment marked "religion" or "church" where they can be considered on an occasional

Sunday morning. That way they are contained and categorized, and therefore domesticated, so their wind and fire do not change and disturb us.

What is the real point? Just this: Inner light shapes our attitudes toward life and people. It is the source from which our actions spring, and it determines how we use the power that is ours. Proverbs says it well:

> Keep your heart with all vigilance;
> for from it flow the springs of life.
> —4:23

Paul's Preoccupation Is God's Power

Paul's prayer for enlightenment has a goal: "that you may know what is . . . the immeasurable greatness of his power in us who believe." Then the sentence goes on to talk about the resurrection of Christ. The energy of Paul's language reveals his preoccupation with God's power. It is a power at fundamental variance with the power everywhere visible in the Roman Empire. This is not to condemn everything Rome stands for, because some of her accomplishments are splendid. The *Pax Romana*, beginning in 27 B.C. with the rule of Augustus, brings two hundred years of peace. The road system and shipping routes cause an ease of transportation unsurpassed for centuries to come. The policy of self-governance for the provinces is enlightened in its day. Art, architecture, and literature flourish. To say the least, it is a time of high civilization. But there is another side to the coin. As Dom Gregory Dix has observed, "The empire was an awe-inspiring achievement, the apotheosis of human power. In the last analysis it represented nothing else but the lust of the flesh and the pride of life triumphant and organized to the point of stability."[3] Rome rules by the power of the sword, subjugating other nations by force. Violence marks the empire indelibly: the spectacle of the Roman circus with its gladiatorial combat and the unleashing of wild beasts on those labeled enemies, the deeply embedded institution of slavery, the assassinations that characterize government power struggles, the inhuman cruelty and decadence of some of the emperors. There is sexuality without limit or restraint and a boundless materialism. It is an empire already past its prime, corrupt in consciousness, preoccupied with physical sensation, exploitive, without a noble vision of God. Tacitus, one of the notable Roman authors of the first century A.D., was not blind to what his nation had become and wrote, "Rome itself, where all the horrible and shameful things in the world collect and find a home."[4]

To this world held in bondage by the iron talons of the Roman eagle, Paul proclaims a new principle of power. It is inseparable from a person, Jesus Christ, and from an event, his resurrection. The reader of these verses in Ephesians 1, especially 19-23, can feel the soul of the apostle lift and soar as it is caught by the rising joy of one whom death's power could not hold captive. Piling one word on top of another, Paul marvels at the power by which God raises Jesus. It is an immeasurable greatness, he says, boundless in accord with the energy of the force of God's strength—that's the way the words come tumbling out in the Greek original. This kind of language is more than exposition, more than explanation, transposing into such poetic passion. It becomes a hymn praising the resurrection and exaltation of Christ, reminiscent of the coronation psalms of the Old Testament. Paul makes his joyful declaration against the dark power of death that holds the world in bondage—death in all of its forms:

war, alienation, chaos, greed. The iron grip of that dark kingdom is broken in Christ's triumph over death. He is now risen and exalted, with a name "above every name that is named." He is the Lord Jesus Christ.

In the final analysis, then, the world does not belong to the spectacular power of Rome, but to the self-giving love of God. If the kingdoms of this fallen world have inevitably exhibited a power that is coercive and forcing obedience, then the kingdom of God exhibits a power more compelling by far, winning our allegiance by its inherent grace and truth. It is in the nature of God's power to gain our willing assent by appealing to the heart and the will. Love knows no other way. What someone demands cannot be given freely, and what is compelled ceases to be love.

The resurrection power of Jesus is not coercive. If it is spectacular, and it certainly is, it is so because of its appeal to the heart. In raising Jesus from death, God makes no abstract statement of power but rather affirms the eternal validity of the self-giving life Jesus lived and the self-giving death he died. Jesus thus bears in himself the nature of God, over which death holds no final authority.

The Passion Is Christ

Key to Paul's thought is the phrase "in the knowledge of him." It is his prayer that his readers will experience an illumination of the heart as the spirit of wisdom inspires a revelation in each person. It is a revelation centered "in the knowledge of him." It is the person of Jesus Christ who defines the nature of the revelation and is the key to its secret. To change the analogy, he is the door through which one walks into a world of light.

When Paul talks about "the knowledge of Christ," he is not talking about information but about relationship. Yes, there are historical facts one should know about Jesus: the things he said and did, the disciples he chose, the events of the last week of his life. But Paul speaks here about the God who is always seeking men and women in the person of the Son, about the effective power of God in Christ through whom persons come into a new relationship and stand on new ground. It is the power of God in this welcomed and indwelling Christ that gives birth to a new creation, so that "the old has passed away, . . . the new has come" (2 Cor. 5:17).

Paul asks three great questions: What is the hope? What are the riches? How great is the power? The answer to each question is found "in the knowledge of him," Jesus! Each is crowded with meaning. Paul says that by knowing Jesus we will know the hope to which he has called us. This does not mean hoping for the best as we wander through the world, hoping our health will hold out, hoping our marriage will hold together, hoping our kids will not go off the deep end, hoping we won't fail in one way or another. The hope of which Paul speaks is indissolubly bound to the presence of Jesus Christ in the heart. In Colossians 1:27 Paul uses the phrase "Christ in you, the hope of glory." It is not this hope or that hope, but *the* hope. Because of the calling of God in Jesus Christ and our positive response to that call, our destiny is forever tied to God's future. We become the children of the kingdom, enlisted to serve the purposes of the Lord of the kingdom.

What are the riches? This is our inheritance as children of God, a kingdom whose wonders "no eye has seen, nor ear heard, nor the heart of man conceived," but which "God has prepared for those who love him" (1 Cor. 2:9).

This is not a future built on speculation about heaven, the world to come, or the far side of death, but a conviction that grows within the Christian because of the presence of the indwelling Christ. The love God demonstrates in him will never let us go.

How great is the power? This is the resurrection power, which says once and for all that life and not death, light and not darkness, love and not despair are the great realities. It is a power which is the inherent energy of the New Testament, responsible for its glorious enthusiasm. Because Christ is risen, it is a new world. Death's dominion over us is broken, and the doors swing open on a world of light. All Christian witness and mission in the world, in the final analysis, moves forward in the power of the resurrection.

The testimony of Paul's life and word is that he met Jesus Christ on the Damascus Road. This encounter is crucial for all he says and does. Is his experience normative for the church in every generation? Our experience may not necessarily repeat the drama of Paul's encounter, but yes, along with everything else we do in the church, we are to maintain a passionate and consistent witness in our own historical context that we are called into relationship with God through a risen Christ. Surely the New Testament is built on the presence and power of a Christ resident within his church and the hearts of his people. What is the church after all, if not the lengthened shadow of Jesus of Nazareth?

> Jesus, Thou Joy of loving hearts,
> Thou Fount of life, Thou Light of men,
> From the best bliss that earth imparts
> We turn unfilled to Thee again.[5]

Notes

1. Abraham J. Heschel, *The Prophets* (New York: Harper & Row, Publishers, 1962), p. 170.
2. Arthur Miller, "The Trouble with Our Country," *San Francisco Chronicle*, 16 June 1968.
3. Dom Gregory Dix, *The Shape of the Liturgy* (London: The Dacre Press, 1945), p. 385-6.
4. F. F. Bruce, *Paul: Apostle of the Heart Set Free* (Grand Rapids, MI: Wm. B. Eerdmans Publishing Co., 1977), p. 442.
5. "Jesus, Thou Joy of Loving Hearts," in *The Hymnal*, no. 354.

II

SENT FOR SALVATION

5. *Jesus Christ Brings Life*

2:1-10

When I was a boy, there was a saying making the rounds that went like this: "That's tough!"

"What's tough?"

"Life's tough."

"What's life?"

"*Life's* a magazine."

"Where do you get it?"

"Down at the corner."

"How much?"

"Ten cents."

"Only got a nickel."

"That's tough."

"What's tough?"

"Life's tough. . . ."

And so on. You can see by the price of the magazine that the saying goes back a few years.

Sometimes we greet friends with the breezy question, "How's life treating you?" It is a question that can solicit a wide range of response. Writers like to tell you what they think about life. The philosopher Thomas Hobbes, for instance, gave as his dark opinion that "the life of man [is] solitary, poor, nasty, brutish, and short."[1] Samuel

Johnson was in a pessimistic mood when he described human life as "everywhere a state in which much is to be endured, and little to be enjoyed."[2]

In the quotations above, the authors focus on the dark side of life. Their attention is absorbed by difficulty, distress, despair, and death. And we all know what they are talking about! They bear witness to a mortality we all share and to the pain of life we all feel. Too concentrated a focus on the dark side, however, can alienate us from life. The things that happen to us and in us can make us so angry, so confused and dead-ended that we want to give up. Some people find it intolerable and take their own lives. No doubt some people reading these lines have wanted to do so. Our struggle with life or against life can bear the fruit of bitterness and cynicism, perhaps so deep that no ray of light seems able to penetrate. Life is going in one direction and we are going in another, fighting the current all the way.

No wonder the everlasting miracle that is life eludes us, although it is all around us. Over our heads an unfathomable mystery, the sky itself stretching out to infinity. Under our feet this planet, once a mass of fiery rock. Over the long centuries it has cooled and brought forth life in staggering abundance, variety, and beauty. And what of us? How could these minds of ours, these human spirits, this individual consciousness have arisen from those primeval seas of molten rock? What dreadful powers does material substance contain that urge it up toward sentient life? Is that the purpose of it all, to form a bridge between inanimate matter and conscious life and soul? For those of us who believe in a Creator God, what profound depths must be in the divine breath giving life to it all! I am suggesting that whenever we are caught in a web of darkness, looking at the wonder of the world can help us.

If we feel hopeless, what of human love? It is real. People do love and are loved. What of our innate hunger for God, the ineradicable impulse to pray, our restless longing for something more than physical bread? But how hard it is to think these thoughts and ask these questions when we are full of pain and doubt. How necessary to ask them and think them nevertheless, for it is always possible for light to penetrate the gloom. God's first creative word rolled back the darkness! "Let there be light," the writer of Genesis records, "and there was light" (Gen. 1:3).

In her book *Pilgrim at Tinker Creek,* Annie Dillard asks these same questions about the wonder of life. She presses us to pause in our rush through the years in order to think and feel deeply, to be more fully aware, not to be anesthetized by the ordinary. She says that each life is a boat floating on the mysterious tide of time, and asks, "Have we rowed out to the thick darkness, or are we all playing pinochle in the bottom of the boat?"[3]

With these thoughts about the dark side and the light side of life as an introduction, we come to this chapter's passage from Ephesians 2:1-10. Paul addresses the most critical question we will ever ask: What is real life? He writes, "And you he made alive, when you were dead through the trespasses and sins in which you once walked, following the course of this world . . . . God, who is rich in mercy, out of the great love with which he loved us, even when we were dead through our trespasses, made us alive together with Christ." If anything is central to Christianity's understanding of life, it is these verses. Do we ask the question, "What does my life mean?" Only when we ask this question will these verses mean anything at all. Otherwise they are little more than religious talk.

Paul begins by saying that it is in the shadow of death that we see the meaning of life. Were there no pain, how could we talk about pleasure? Were there no night, how could we describe the day? Were there no evil, how could we choose the good? Were there no death, would life be precious? Scripture and human experience know full well the reality of "the valley of the shadow of death" (Psalm 23:4). The psalmist asked, "What man can live and never see death? Who can deliver his soul from the power of Sheol?" (89:48). Hebrews' phrase, memorable indeed, declares, "it is appointed for men (humankind) to die" (9:27). Everybody knows that. We may evade it, fear it, deny it by the way we live, but we all know it. Jack Benny used to say that if he couldn't take it with him he wasn't going, but he went anyway. That's what it means to be human. It is against this background of our mortality that Paul writes to the Ephesians, "You he made alive, when you were dead." If that doesn't pique our curiosity, nothing will.

Paul names three things that belong to the realm of death: sin, Satan, and self. He says that we are dead because of our sins. Sin is a more profound reality than we often think. It is more than the bad word prompted by anger or frustration, more than the bad habits with which we may struggle, more than our unkindness to others. It is not to be equated with "foible" or individual bad deeds any of us may do. We rob it of its dimensions when we limit its dominion in human life. It is a state of being, a land in which we dwell, a kingdom in which we hold citizenship, the kingdom of death. There are two words in this passage that describe the nature of sin and are central to Paul's theology. Neither refers to bad deeds primarily but rather to a state of being. The first word is translated as "trespasses" and means "to slip, fall, or stumble." The second word is translated as "sins" and means "to fall short of the mark." It is the word used when an archer's arrow doesn't reach the target. Both words have the core idea of failure. A lot of us have the feeling that we are just not making it, do we not? There is something momentous missing, some mysterious hidden fire that lies near us but out of reach and awareness.

My step-father retired in 1963. He was sitting in a chair in the living room one day, and he asked a question I will not forget if I live to be a hundred. It was addressed as much to himself and his undiscovered God as it was to me: "Why have I been such a failure?" What did he mean? He was not referring to the facts that he had done a simple laborer's work all his life, had never made a lot of money, or had never gone to high school. Instead, there was a vacuum that had never been filled and a hunger that had never been satisfied. It was a hunger for life in a fullness only guessed at by the emptiness within. He had done a lot of good things, been an honest and responsible man, but life had eluded him. His individual sins weren't that important, only reflections of his failure to find life. The definition of sin that fitted him best was "falling short, losing the way."

The second thing that this passage says about death is that it has a ruler, one who is named, ominously enough, "the prince of the power of the air." That's quite a title! Sometimes he is called "The Prince of Darkness." Any writer is faced with opposite tensions when commenting on such a phrase, either to make too much of it or to make too little of it. The Bible does not make too much of it; that is, it does not dwell on the devil or draw topographical maps of hell. Some religions have a detailed demonology, but not Christianity. Evil power is personified in scripture, but the devil is not all-powerful, nor is the Bible preoccupied with him.

On the other hand, there is a tension pulling us toward making too little of it, toward discounting personified evil as an ancient superstition, passing quickly over such fanciful titles as "the prince of the power of the air." It may be, however, that a scientific age does not know more about the nature of ultimate reality than earlier generations. What is our experience of evil? is the question to raise, for that is the question the Bible raises. Put aside for a moment the menacing personification of evil as "The Prince of Darkness." How do we meet evil in our lives and in our world? As a power! What kind of power? A power that seeks to dissipate all order, beauty, and love, sucking everything into the abyss of nothingness; a power that seeks to waste substance and to breed chaos; a power that seeks to tear down, to destroy, and to negate. Senseless violence, war, murder, torture, concentration camps, exploitation, the manipulation of others for our own ends, all these things are the signature of evil. It is whatever seeks to prevent God's will from being done, a will that is known in the things that make for love, freedom, order, beauty, faith, and joy. Evil meets us as a power that is sometimes so menacing that we can feel its breath on the back of our neck, or watch it stride across our world. Perhaps that is why Walter Wink writes: "The demonic confronts us as a single realm, personal and collective, inner and outer, archetypal and institutional. It is the experience of the *unity* of the forces of the fragmentation, and not religious obscurantism, that requires us to acknowledge the Prince of demons and his kingdom of death."[4]

The third mark of evil in human experience is living for the self alone. This is the temptation to rewrite the Lord's Prayer to say, "Hallowed be my name, my kingdom come, my will be done." What is life all about? My nurture, care, and feeding! Peter Marin, looking at contemporary American culture, writes about "the world view emerging among us centered solely on the self and with individual survival as its sole good."[5] The truth of the matter is that the human ego is boundless. No matter how much affirmation is poured in, how many material advantages are gained, or how successful we are in piling up honors, we are never satisfied. We become slaves to our own selfishness. It is not until we discover Jesus' insight about self-giving that we begin to know what real life is: "Whoever would save his life will lose it; and whoever loses his life for my sake and the gospel's will save it" (Mark 8:35).

Enough about sin and death! These verses in Ephesians 2 are about life. It is because Paul writes about life against the backdrop of sin and death that he speaks with such joy. These words pour forth out of an enraptured heart. Having spoken about the dark ruler of the kingdom of death, Paul launches into his song of praise with two stacatto words: "But God"! We were spiritually dead, *but God!* We did not know the answers, *but God!* We could not find the way, *but God!* We were captive to the prince of power of the air, *but God!* We knew no way of living except for our own advantage, *but God!* Then the affirmations come tumbling out: "God, who is rich in mercy, . . . the great love with which he loved us . . . made us alive together with Christ . . . and raised us up with him . . . the immeasurable riches of his grace in kindness toward us."

There is no doubt about Paul's answer to life's meaning. He has a ready answer, a passionate answer. For Paul, life's meaning is to be found in the Christ whom God raised up from death. As with Paul, so with Christians across the centuries. In whatever generation Christians read these words, they intuitively respond: "We know what you mean, we hear what you say, we feel what you feel. The truth that has planted itself in your heart plants itself in ours and we say with you, 'To me to live is Christ'" (Phil. 1:21). In this the church is one in all times and places. Isn't it true, after all, that down at the core of what we are is a hunger for life, not necessarily a better life in material things, but a hunger for a fuller degree of life. We want to drink deeply, to experience fully, to know more profoundly what it means to live. The answer, says Paul, is Christ.

There are those who have spent a lifetime in the Christian church without feeling the surge of life that permeates this passage. No bells ring when the words are read. Somehow we have not made the transition from Christianity as religion to Christianity as life. Maybe the intuititive and spiritual sides of our nature are not developed in us as they are in other people who are nourished by the same words that leave us untouched. But that side of our nature is not absent and can be cultivated.

Let me tell you about the negative side of religion: It can keep us from encounter with God. We can be so wrapped up in the church as institution that we lose touch with the church as wind and fire of God. The mechanics, the administration, the committee meetings, the inevitable church fights, the politics absorb us to such an extent that we do not comprehend or perhaps do not risk the incandescent touch of the Spirit. The church can become a line of defense against God.

Here is an illustration of the difference between religion and life. I am a fisherman. I often tell people, "I am off to pursue the wily trout." Several summers ago on an August evening with the sun just set, my son and I were on a sweeping bend of the Yellowstone River just below Livingston, Montana. We were alone, just the two of us, when a substantial rainbow trout took my streamer. Have you ever seen a rainbow jump, seen the spray of water, colors glistening? By nature this great fish runs and leaps and runs again, often tail-walking down the current. When you slip a net over such a grand fighter, feel the weight of the fish, see it up close, well, that's fishing! But there's another way to experience the trout. You can go to a laboratory and take a trout out of a jar of Formalin. There it is, rainbow trout, no doubt about it; real fish, no doubt about it! But the jar smells terrible, and the fish is stiff and colorless. You can study it, record in a book the nature of the fins and the gill structure, and you are right. You have incontrovertable facts about the nature of the fish. But have you experienced a rainbow trout? There is but a single difference: One is alive and the other is dead!

The analogy is plain. Is the Christ of whom Paul speaks alive in our experience? Has religion, however well-intentioned, kept Christ shrouded in its institutional trappings? Is he captured in an impenetrable Bible like a fly in amber? Is he cold and distant like an ancient creed? To whatever extent this is true, the life in Christianity loses its ability to touch and change our human lives. It is a living Christ present in the church and in the heart, a Christ who is Companion for all our journeys, of whom Paul speaks: "God, who is rich in mercy, out of the great love with which he loved us, even when we were dead through our trespasses, made us alive together with Christ (by grace you have been saved), and raised us up with him."

Notes

1. Thomas Hobbs, *Leviathan, Part 1* (Chicago: Henry Regnery Company, 1956), p. 118.
2. Samuel Johnson, *The History of Rasselas, Prince of Abyssinia,* in M. H. Abrams, et al., eds., *The Norton Anthology of English Literature,* vol. 1 (New York: W. W. Norton & Company, 1968), p. 1824.
3. Annie Dillard, p. 8.
4. Walter Wink, *Unmasking the Powers* (Philadelphia: Fortress Press, 1986), p. 68.
5. Peter Marin, "The New Narcissism," *Harper's Magazine,* October 1975, p. 46.

6. Jesus Christ Brings Reconciliation

2:11-18

Reconciliation is not a word we use with any frequency, and therefore it belongs more to our reading vocabulary than our speaking vocabulary. Occasionally we talk about reconciling a column of figures, which means checking one column against another for accuracy. Sometimes we say that "John and Mary Smith" have been reconciled, which means that after a period of estrangement differences have been settled and the relationship restored.

I looked up the word *reconcile* in *The Oxford Dictionary of Quotations* and found four entries, only one of which was really quotable: "Strange to see how a good dinner and feasting reconciles everybody." This was a diary entry made by Samuel Pepys on Nov. 9, 1665, no doubt after a robust evening.[1]

While the word does not seem to be highly important in the English language or in our every-day speech, it is a significant word in the letters of Paul. The Greek word Paul uses and which our English texts translate "reconcile" comes from a root word that means "to change," as in altering the appearance of something or in changing one's clothes. In secular Greek the word Paul uses in our text means "changing money." Since language develops with time, it later acquired a wider sense of exchanging one thing for another and finally came to mean "to change enmity for friendship." When Paul is writing, the characteristic use of the word in his culture means "the bringing together of people who have been estranged."[2] This is the meaning of *reconcile* as Paul uses it and as it is translated in our English Bibles.

This second half of Ephesians 2 "is the key and high point of the whole epistle." Markus Barth says that in one of the excellent commentaries on Ephesians.[3] Moreover, in this key passage in the book is a key word, the one we have been talking about: *reconcile*. We can say it is the most important word in the most important passage in Ephesians. This is because it describes the action of God through which we find forgiveness and are brought into right relationship so that we begin to know the meaning of the worship, love, and service of God.

For the sake of order and clarity in the development of this text, here are two ideas: exclusion, inclusion.

Exclusion

Paul's words are dramatic: "Remember that you were at that time separated from Christ, alienated from the commonwealth of Israel, and strangers to the covenants of promise, having no hope and without God in the world." That's exclusion! It's a bleak picture he paints, and a barren landscape he sketches in as background. These Gentile members of the Ephesian church, all of whom had worshiped the pagan deities of the day, had been far, far away from the God of grace whom Paul often calls "The God and Father of our Lord Jesus Christ." They were outside, they were distant, they were alienated, they were strangers.

No commentator, let alone preacher, could pass this by without observing that exclusion from relationship with God is not a theological category but a condition of the inner life. Paul describes this condition with a dark word, *alienation,* implying that people are not simply unaware of God, or unconcerned with God, or unchurched and therefore ignorant of God but are alienated. There is a basic disharmony, a distance maintained across the years. Just mention prayer or confession or the presence of God or the love of Christ and a lot of people start running to meet appointments they have just remembered.

To be more specific, one of the marks of our exclusion from God is guilt. This is a universal experience, the conviction that something is wrong and needs to be made right. Since the beginning of time, men and women have felt in debt to whatever gods they recognized and out of a restless conscience have made their sacrifices for forgiveness and restoration to favor. Literature bears witness to the guilt we feel. In *Sea Dreams,* for instance, Tennyson writes:

> he that wrongs his friend
> Wrongs himself more, and ever bears about
> A silent court of justice in his breast,
> Himself the judge and jury, and himself
> The prisoner at the bar, ever condemn'd,
> And that drags down his life.[4]

If physical pain is an alarm telling us that some part of the body is suffering distress and needs attention, then guilt is a spiritual alarm telling us that there is trouble in the inner life.

A second mark of our exclusion from God is anxiety. If guilt worries about the things that have happened in the past, then anxiety worries about the things that may happen in the future. Anxiety tries to control the uncontrollable. We can fret away our days and nights over things that very well may not happen. No matter how tight we set our jaw muscles, no matter what magnitude our fretting, it has no effect on the airplane on which our friend or family member is flying. The plane's safety is not affected in the least by our anxiety. The only thing affected is our cardio-vascular system.

We need a little humor about our anxiety. None of us escapes entirely. Snoopy says that when something bad is going to happen to you there shouldn't be any night before. A. A. Milne wrote:

> There was once an old sailor my grandfather knew
> Who had so many things he wanted to do
> That, whenever he thought it was time to begin,
> He couldn't because of the state he was in.[5]

The state we are in causes the writing of 144 million new prescriptions a year for psychotropic drugs, including antidepressants and tranquilizers.[6] Half of these prescriptions are for Valium and Librium.

A third mark of our exclusion from God is emptiness. It is one of the gray shapes that haunt out lives, leaving us restless and unfulfilled. Carl Jung, after having counselled hundreds of people, observed, "About a third of my cases are suffering from no clinically definable neurosis, but from the senselessness and emptiness of their lives . . . the general neurosis of our time."[7] Perhaps the frenetic hunger for drugs, the excessive use of alcohol, the pleasure chase, and the fever with which so many pursue material security are ways we try to satisfy the emptiness within. Maybe beneath it all we are searching for the lost music, the harmony and the wholeness that, I think, cannot be found outside the love of God.

Human experience bears out what the text is saying, that we feel ourselves to be excluded from relationship with God. This manifests itself as guilt, anxiety, and emptiness. It is as if some great discovery has eluded us.

Inclusion

Paul uses an illustration to clarify what he means by his twin themes of alienation and reconciliation. He says that Christ "has broken down the dividing wall." That is, whatever was causing the separation between God and us has been removed. One has to have a picture of the Jerusalem Temple with its four surrounding court enclosures to feel the impact of Paul's statement. First and farthest away was the Court of the Gentiles, next the Court of the Women, third the Court of the Sons of Israel, and finally the Court of the Priests, which opened into the Temple itself. Part way back in the Temple a heavy curtain hung from ceiling to floor, hiding a space called the Holy of Holies. Here, Israel believed, the very presence of God dwelt. So sacred was this enclosure that only one man was permitted to enter, the high priest, and he could enter only once a year on the Day of Atonement. On the fringes of his robe were little bells, lest coming in silently he catch God unaware and be struck dead meeting Yahweh face to face. Had not God said, "You cannot see my face; for man shall not see me and live" (Ex. 33:20)? Talk about the majesty of God!

No Gentile was allowed to proceed beyond the first court. A marble wall, intricately carved, divided the Court of the Gentiles from the rest of the courts and from the Temple itself. Signs were set into the wall at regular intervals warning Gentiles to go no further. One of these signs was discovered in an archaeological dig in 1871. It reads, "Let no one of any other nation come within the fence and barrier around the Holy Place. Whosoever will be taken doing so will himself be responsible for the fact that his death will ensue."[8] This wall, obviously, excluded Gentiles from the presence of God. When Paul writes to the Ephesians that they were separated, alienated, and strangers, this was surely the image he had in mind. It is, indeed, a dramatic image! Shut out from the presence of God! The language that follows is just as dramatic, and Paul introduces it with two familiar code words: "But now!" These are words of contrast, staccato words used by Paul to reveal his amazement at the grace of God. You Gentiles, you were without hope and without God, *"but now* in Christ Jesus you who once were far off have been brought near in the blood of Christ."

If the words of exclusion were dark and foreboding, then the words of inclusion are full of light and promise. Once more the soul of the apostle soars as he describes the Christ who breaks down the wall of separation and ushers forgiven sinners into the presence of God. Paul's descriptive language continues to borrow imagery from the Temple and its precincts as he tells the Ephesians what Christ has done. Picture the rich and solemn worship at the Temple in Jerusalem on the Day of Atonement. Perhaps you know it by the Hebrew name, *Yom Kippur.* The courts of the Temple are crowded with people, each court on a higher level than the one behind it so that everyone can see what is happening in the Court of the Priests, which opens into the Temple. All eyes are fixed on the great altar of sacrifice, just in front of the Temple doors. Here the high priest raises the knife to sacrifice a lamb for the sins of the nation. Then he carries a bowl of the blood inside the temple, entering through the curtain into the Holy of Holies, where he sprinkles the blood in the presence of God. He may not enter this space without blood, sign and symbol that Israel knows how far she falls short of who God is and what God wills. She gives God her most precious gift, life, acknowledging her distance and her desire to be brought near.

Just so, says Paul, Jesus is the lamb of God. He gives his most precious gift, his life, that we may be brought near to God. Through his sacrifice our sins are forgiven and forgotten forever! The gulf between us and God, visible in our guilt, anxiety, and emptiness, is bridged. We who were excluded are included, we who were strangers are fellow-citizens, we who were distant have been brought near.

What does it all feel like internally? What is the spiritual and personal dynamic? The war is over! Fear of God or hostility toward God are dissolved. Alienation is replaced by reconciliation. The emptiness is being filled by a loving presence difficult to describe but impossible to mistake. Paul sums it up in a phrase, "[Christ] is our peace." It is a peace that is personal but that extends from the individual. Because it is life-changing, even revolutionary in our own experience, it spreads out like ripples in a pool until the scope of the peace Christ brings is universal. Jew and Gentile stand on common ground, both finding forgiveness and access to God. Paul says that Christ makes both Jew and Gentile one. He says that in Christ God brings hostility to an end.

The peace of Christ, then, is not simply passive, a

personal release from anxiety. It is active, affecting the nature of all our relationships, both with God and with neighbors everywhere. If religion has been a dull and heavy thing without wings, without conscious knowledge of the love of God, now a new and living relationship is born. That relationship spills over into every human relationship so that we begin to see Christ in those around us. Being forgiven, we find it easier to forgive. Being loved, we find it easier to love. Being at peace with God, we find it easier to be at peace with others. Because we are included by God, we find it harder to exclude people around us.

In France during the First World War, some soldiers brought a dead comrade to be buried in a French cemetery. The priest had to explain that this was a Roman Catholic cemetery and asked if their fallen comrade was a baptized Catholic. They said they didn't know, and the priest said he was sorry but he could not permit the burial in the churchyard. So the soldiers took their friend and buried him just outside the fence in unconsecrated ground. The next day they came back to lay some flowers on the grave, but could not find it. They knew it had been only six feet outside the fence. No fresh dirt could be found there. As they stood there astonished, the priest came up. He told them he had been greatly troubled by his refusal yesterday, so early that morning he had dug up the posts of the fence and moved it to include the body of their friend.[9]

Christians are committed to inclusion. We break down walls that keep people out: social walls like the wrong side of the tracks, political walls like the Iron Curtain, economic walls like the haves and have-nots, racial walls like apartheid, walls that exclude and shut out. We could well quote Robert Frost's line, "Something there is that doesn't love a wall."[10] Having peace with God, we become peacemakers everywhere. Being reconciled to God, we become agents of reconciliation.

Notes

1. *The Oxford Dictionary of Quotations*, 3rd ed. (Oxford: Oxford University Press, 1979), p. 372.
2. William Barclay, *More New Testament Words* (New York: Harper & Row, Publishers, 1958), p. 104.
3. Markus Barth, *Ephesians: Introduction, Translation and Commentary on Chapters 1-3*, vol. 34 of *The Anchor Bible* (New York: Doubleday & Company, 1974), p. 275.
4. *Alfred Lord Tennyson*, "Sea Dreams," in *The Poetic and Dramatic Works of Alfred Lord Tennyson* (Boston: Houghton, Mifflin and Company, 1898), p. 255.
5. A. A. Milne, "The Old Sailor," in *Now We Are Six* (New York: E.P. Dutton & Company, 1927, reprinted 1961), p. 38.
6. Kenneth R. Pelletier, *Mind as Healer, Mind as Slayer* (New York: Dell Publishing Co., Inc., 1977), p. 20.
7. Carl G. Jung, *Modern Man in Search of a Soul* (New York: Harcourt, Brace & World, 1933), p. 61.
8. William Barclay, *The Letters to the Galatians and Ephesians* (Philadelphia: Westminster Press, 1958), pp. 130-1.
9. Ibid., p. 135.
10. Robert Frost, "Mending Wall," in *The Poetry of Robert Frost* (New York: Holt, Rinehart and Winston, 1969), p. 33.

7. Jesus Christ Brings Meaning

2:19-22

Most of us have lived a wide variety of experience. Birth and death, marriage and divorce, success and failure, sorrow and loss, I have seen a lot of life. One night I got a call from Phyllis, a friend. She said, "Henry is going to kill himself!" I went over to the house where the couple lived with their three children and found Henry nervously pacing the floor. He looked like the last rose of summer. Lighting a cigarette, he said to me, "What shall I do, work another day to eat another day to live another day to work another day?" He was saying, "My life is not making any sense, so why go on?" It was a question about meaning.

Another man, a black industrial worker in his early forties, put it this way: "I'm working in the business, hard. And I'm getting older, and the energy I started with is running out. Sooner or later I'm not going to be able to work as hard, and I really haven't gotten anyplace. As you get older, you begin to think of yourself as a man in a hurry. The years are going by, and you want to know your life meant something."[1]

Loren Eiseley makes a particularly poignant statement about meaning in an autographical book called *All the*

Strange Hours: "We, she and I, were close to being one now, lying like the skeletons of last year's leaves in a fence corner. And it was all nothing. Nothing, do you understand? All the pain, all the anguish. Nothing. We were, both of us, merely the debris life always leaves in its passing."[2]

Everyone wants to live with meaning! As I counsel and interact with people, as I take the pulse of my own life, I am convinced that all of us want to make sense out of our days and years. Isn't that one of the functions of our mortality—to point out our limited supply of time so that we are forced to ask, "What's it all about?" How anesthetized becomes the inner life if we fail to ask essential questions about meaning. In *Pilgrim at Tinker Creek,* Annie Dillard writes of a woman who said to her, "Seem like we're just set down here and don't nobody know why."[3]

Enough introduction! "Jesus Christ Brings Meaning," the title of this chapter, is an affirmation that takes shape in Ephesians 2:19-22. Here Paul talks about the church as a building and singles out three essential parts of its construction: the foundation, the keystone, and the building blocks. We will look at each in turn.

The Foundation

Let's put these verses in context. In the first eighteen verses of this second chapter, Paul has used some arresting language. He tells the Ephesians that they were formerly dead in their sins. He says they were "separated from Christ, alienated from the commonwealth of Israel, and strangers to the covenants of promise, having no hope and without God in the world" (v. 12). It is a catalogue of exclusion. Paul goes on to speak of the reconciling work of Christ and the inclusion of the whole

Gentile world in God's love. Verse 19 is the soaring summation of the whole chapter: "So then you are no longer strangers and sojourners, but you are fellow citizens with the saints and members of the household of God." This grand affirmation of the loving acceptance of God is a statement about meaning. No longer strangers, no longer aliens, no longer waifs in a hostile world but now citizens at home in God's house. It is a wonderfully warm and comforting affirmation. In the three verses that follow, Paul expands his thought. He has mentioned "the household of God" and now begins to describe the church as the spiritual house, the dwelling place of God. It is an impressive image of the nature of the church. Every building, of course, begins with a foundation. As he thinks about the growing churches scattered around the Mediterranean world, Paul begins to draw out the analogy. Without a foundation, nothing else really matters and nothing will endure. That solid base upon which the church is built, its dependable grounding, is the apostles and prophets. This is surely an Old Testament image and a New Testament image joined to form a single truth. There is harmony between the two. Each is essential. The apostles are the band of disciples chosen by Jesus, and Paul is the apostle to the Gentiles uniquely chosen through his Damascus Road vision of a risen Christ, by whom he is called and commissioned. The prophets are Old Testament figures like Moses, Isaiah, and Jeremiah. How do they form a foundation? It is their experience of God and their service in his purposes that makes them prototypes of faith and therefore foundational for all who would know, love, and serve God. They bear witness that midway in their life's journey they have been met unforgettably by the presence of the Eternal

One, the Almighty. Like Moses keeping the sheep of his father-in-law, Jethro, in the wilderness of Midian, or like Peter casting his nets in Galilee, they were pursuing the ordinary when they heard a call so extraordinary that they were never the same again. God became known, set them to a task, and promised to be with them. This pattern is so unmistakable that one can define the Bible as the lengthened shadow of great experiences of God. Abram in Ur of the Chaldees, Jacob at Bethel, Moses at the burning bush, Joshua in the conquest of Canaan, David in his songs and his battles, Solomon at the dedication of the Temple, Isaiah's great vision of God recorded in the sixth chapter of his book, the resurrection appearances in the gospels, and Paul's conversion are all uniform in their pattern, though different in their detail. God calls and commissions for service. The apostles and prophets are the foundation of the church.

Upon what foundation do we contemporary people build our lives? What is it that informs who we are, instills our values, and gives direction to our living? Do we draw our essential meaning by osmosis from our national cultures? Is it our peer group and our desire to fit in that shapes who we are? Who are we anyway? It does not take an unusual degree of perception to conclude that we live in a society that is awash with contradictory, confusing, and illusory answers to our deepest needs. Modern culture says:

Make money, that's the answer,
Make love, that's the answer.
Make a name for yourself, that's the answer.
Make big waves, that's the answer.
Make whoopee, that's the answer.
Everyone for herself/himself, and devil take the hindmost.

None of these things separately or together will give us what we seek and perpetually hunger for, a sense of meaning. We can wander around a lifetime without ever finding a central value around which to order our days and years. We need a foundation on which to stand. Christians find theirs in the God revealed in Old Testament and New and uniquely in Jesus.

Keystone

"Christ Jesus himself being the keystone" (AP). The usual translations say "cornerstone." Why change to "keystone"? The cornerstone, after all, sits directly on the foundation holding two walls together, giving them their angle. It is the first and most important stone laid, the one on which all the others depend and to which they relate. Is not Christ the cornerstone who binds together in himself both Jew and Gentile, Old Testament and New, promise and fulfillment, law and grace? Peter writes, "Come to him, to that living stone, . . . and like living stones be yourselves built into a spiritual house. . . . For it stands in Scripture: 'Behold, I am laying in Zion a stone, a cornerstone chosen and precious' " (1 Pet. 2:4-6).

This is a striking metaphor. It is the accepted translation of Ephesians 2:20. But consider *keystone*. A keystone is the wedge-shaped piece of rock at the crown of an arch locking all the other pieces in place. It literally holds up the arch. Pennsylvania, for instance, is called, "The Keystone State." Originally this was a geographic reference, since Pennsylvania was located in a key position between the northern and southern states.

Whenever I begin to focus on a word like this in the interpretation of a passage, I am tempted to get some mileage out of my many years of language study, elaborating lengthy details. Quotes from the early church fathers and ancient prayers from the synagogue lie ready at hand in my library. The reader will be spared these academics, however, and be asked to consider this: Christ is not only the one upon whom the church rests but also the one toward whom the church moves. As the stones in an arch lean upon the keystone, so the living stones of the church lean upon Jesus Christ for strength and support. Ephesians 1:22 says that God has made Christ "the head over all things for the church, which is his body." This is a parallel image. As the whole church body grows toward its head, so the individual stones in an arch reach up toward the keystone. The apostles and prophets are the foundation; Jesus Christ is the keystone.

A number of observations flow from the image of Christ as keystone. If indeed he informs and rules the church from the past, if his life, death, and resurrection are foundational and historic, as they are, this by no means exhausts who Christ is for the church. One of the most frequently quoted and deeply treasured verses of the New Testament is Matthew 18:20: "Where two or three are gathered in my name, there am I in the midst of them." Jesus Christ belongs to the past and also to the living present.

In its celebration of the Eucharist across the generations, the church has always proclaimed that Christ is present in the breaking of the bread. And what comfort and assurance to Christians is that last sentence in Matthew's Gospel: Jesus' promise, "I am with you always." Still the meaning of Christ for the church is not exhausted, for he stands not only in the past sending the church, and not only in the present strengthening the church, but in the future summoning the church. One of the memorable parables of the New Testament pictures a wedding party awaiting the bridegroom, his delay, and his arrival (Matt. 25:1-13), making the poignant assertion that Christ is yet to come. "Be faithful unto death, and I will give you the crown of life," are words of the Christ of Revelation summoning the church to steadfast faith in the midst of suffering (2:10). One of the church's hymns speaks of Christ both present and future when it says, "Christ is the Path, and Christ the Prize."[4] We confess that Christ is the future toward which we move whenever we say that he is "the Alpha and the Omega, the first and the last, the beginning and the end" (Rev. 22:13).

These many references give the sense that *keystone* gives: Christ is not only foundation upon which the church rests but horizon toward which the church moves. St. Jerome puts it all in a sentence when he says that Christ "is the foundation and top because in him the church is founded and completed."[5]

Building Blocks

Paul concludes his thought by saying that in Christ, the keystone, "the whole structure is joined together and grows into a holy temple in the Lord; in whom you also are built into it for a dwelling place of God in the Spirit."

It's hard for people to visualize the church as anything but a building. "Good old First Church," they say, "it's been there for years. Sure could use a coat of paint right now. Why shucks, if you knew some of the things that have gone on there you just wouldn't believe it!" That's right. People find it hard to think of the church as anything but a building, a physical structure. They talk about going *to* the church or being *in* the church. The only time they use the word *church* to mean "people" is when they say they were offended *by* the church. That usually translates to mean the pastor or one of the lay leaders.

But this text of ours is talking about the church as a spiritual house of God, a dwelling place for God. That means the people themselves, not the building itself. God, by the Spirit, lives in people who are living in response to God's call and commission. Avery and Marsh's popular song hits the nail on the head: "I am the church! You are the church! We are the church together! All who follow Jesus, All around the world! Yes, we're the church together."[6]

The descriptive image of the church created by Paul in this second chapter of Ephesians is vibrant and alive. The church, in its essential nature, is a spiritual house of God built of living stones. This makes it difficult to choose only a few comments. If the church is composed of people, then it is a human church that is far from perfect. It is not angels who are built into the church but people. They will make mistakes, they will misuse authority, they will break God's laws, they will offend others. But at their best it will be evident that they have submitted their lives to the Master Craftsman for restoration and renewal. Sometimes it is more revealing to ask where persons have come from than to ask where they are. An unmistakable fragrance will permeate a church that is being built into "a dwelling place of God in the Spirit."

Paul says that "the whole structure is joined together." He means at least that the growth of the community of faith is decisive for the authenticity of the church. It is certainly true that each Christian is "a dwelling place of God in the Spirit," but the church will wither away if it is merely a collection of pious individuals. When our lives are joined together in love for God and in a common journey of faith, then the gospel happens in our midst. It is surely true that we are the church together or we are not the church at all. As we learn to accept each other, struggle with each other, love each other, work with each other in our mutual allegiance to the Lord of the church, grace overtakes us so that we say with Jacob, "Surely the Lord is in this place; and I did not know it." "How awesome is this place! This is none other than the house of God" (Gen. 28:16-17).

How real is this to us who sit in the churches and serve in the churches? Is our shared commitment to Jesus Christ our center of meaning? To what extent do the contemporary values of our modern culture shape us more than our Christian faith?

Is the church one more cultural commitment among many that prove our good citizenship? What are the real energies that shape us? Power over others, material well-being, a place high up on the social register or the corporate pyramid, being a *femme fatale* or the laid-back driver of hot sports car? Who are we anyway? We will never ask a more important question, nor will we ever make a more important response than the one every church member has been asked to make: "Jesus Christ is my Lord and Savior." To get that center steady is to find meaning and to make sense out of all the scattered pieces of our lives.

Notes

1. Maggie Scarf, "Husbands in Crisis," *McCall's Magazine,* June 1972, p. 122.
2. Loren Eiseley, *All the Strange Hours* (New York: Charles Scribner's Sons, 1975), p. 25.
3. Annie Dillard, p. 2.
4. "Fight the Good Fight," *The Hymnal,* no. 270.
5. Markus Barth, p. 319.
6. Richard Avery and Donald Marsh, "We Are the Church," in *Songs for the Easter People* (Port Jervis, NY: Proclamation Productions, Inc., 1973), p. 20.

III

SENT FOR THE WORLD

8. The Universal Christ

3:1-6

This passage from Ephesians 3 makes as clear a claim as any that Paul is uniquely "the apostle to the Gentiles." The primary meaning of "apostle" given by *The New Westminster Dictionary of the Bible* is this: "One of the men selected by Jesus to be eyewitnesses of the events of his life, to see him after his resurrection, and to testify to mankind concerning him."[1] Paul fits this definition, but in an unusual way. He never saw Jesus "in the days of his flesh," but rather, he experienced a life-transforming vision of the risen Christ on the road to Damascus. His commission to the Gentiles is inseparable from that conversion, as he relates to King Agrippa:

> At midday, O king, I saw on the way a light from heaven, brighter than the sun, shining round me and those who journeyed with me. And when we had all fallen to the ground, I heard a voice saying to me in the Hebrew language, "Saul, Saul, why do you persecute me? It hurts you to kick against the goads." And I said, "Who are you, Lord?" And the Lord said, "I am Jesus whom you are persecuting. But rise and stand upon your feet; for I have appeared to you for this purpose, to appoint you to serve

> and bear witness to . . . the Gentiles . . . to open their eyes, that they may turn from darkness to light."
>
> —Acts 26:13-18

Paul's call to be an apostle and his claim to apostolic authority rest on that event that changed his life forever. "Am I not an apostle?" he writes. "Have I not seen Jesus our Lord?" (1 Cor. 9:1).

The Jewish race of Paul's day divided the world in two. While ethnically there were Greeks, Romans, and Jews, as well as a number of other nationalities beyond the Mediterranean world, religiously there were only Jews and Gentiles. The Jews were God's chosen people; all the rest were cursed and lived in darkness. In view of such a mind-set, passages like this one in Ephesians brought consternation and struggle to the Jewish people. How could it be that God's love embraces all—that it is in fact universal? Where is the uniqueness of Israel? The Gentiles have always fought against God's people, so where is the justice of God? Yet Paul, caught in the machinery of Roman law, tells King Agrippa how he met a risen Christ, God's Messiah, and was commissioned to bring the gospel of God's acceptance to the Gentile world.

Captive to Christ's Power

The text we study in this chapter begins with the words "I, Paul, a prisoner for Christ Jesus on behalf of you Gentiles." As he writes, Paul is probably in Rome, chained to the wrist of a guard, waiting trial before Nero. He had gone to Jerusalem against the best advice of believers in Caesarea in order to address the Council of the Apostles. He wished to tell them how mightily God was moving among the Gentiles and to convince them that Gentiles as well as Jews were called by God to faith in the Messiah. He was able to address and convince the council. However, when Paul entered the temple to worship, his enemies stirred up the people. They were on the point of killing him when he was rescued by Roman legionnaires. He was accused of bringing a Gentile into the Temple against Jewish law, an Ephesian named Trophimus, and of being an agitator who would cause endless trouble for Roman authority. Finally, in order to escape the plots of Jewish enemies against his life, he appealed his case to Caesar. Such an appeal could not be denied him, since he was a Roman citizen. This is why he is under house arrest in Rome bound arm to arm with a soldier. He is not in a dungeon, nor subsisting on a bread and water diet, but he is a prisoner nonetheless. Should Paul escape, the guard would pay with his life. Strange then that in these circumstances Paul does not call himself the prisoner of Rome, but rather the prisoner of Jesus Christ.

Perhaps it's all in the point of view, in the way you think about yourself. It's in your self-consciousness. Paul does not regard himself as the victim of circumstance; he does not complain about the slings and arrows of outrageous fortune; he does not wring his hands and say, "If I had only stayed away from Jerusalem like they told me to, I wouldn't be in this fix!" He is not a man wandering through the world hoping for the best, but a man with a mission, a man committed to a vision, a man held by a loyalty far more important than his own life. One fancies him rising to his feet, head held high, with pride and passion mingled in his eyes as he says, "I, Paul, a prisoner for Christ Jesus."

Surely Paul, in this magnificent declaration, is asking his readers to respond to the question, "Under whose authority do you live?" When life's troubles seem like a surrounding sea, as they do for him, he is asking, "Where is your anchor? To what extent does Jesus Christ inform and shape your life story?" Paul's reply is normative for Christians: "I, Paul, a prisoner for Christ Jesus."

Receptive to Christ's Secret

This brings us to a second major claim by Paul in this text. Not only is he captive to Christ's power, but he also remains open to Christ's mystery. He writes, "You have heard of the stewardship of God's grace that was given to me for you, how the mystery was made known to me by revelation. . . . When you read this you can perceive my insight into the mystery of Christ . . . as it has now been revealed." *Mystery* is a word to which my own heart is receptive. It is congenial to my nature, eliciting immediate emotional response. These verses, then, are appealing to me personally. I agree with Amos Wilder when he says, "The human heart would suffocate if it were restricted to logic."[2] Paul is telling the Ephesians about a mystery that was made known to him, a secret hidden in the heart of God from the beginning of the world. It is not a secret that could ever be discovered by human wisdom, but, like the presence of God, it has been awaiting the time of revelation. It is a secret woven into the divine purposes, inseparable from the will of God. And now the time of disclosure has come! *The New English Bible* translates Paul's words like this: "In former generations this was not disclosed to the human race; but now it has been revealed by inspiration to his dedicated apostles and prophets." Paul knows himself to be one of those apostles—in fact *the* apostle to the Gentiles. He intends his writing to be dramatic, since he himself is a central player in the drama.

And what is this secret? What have the long ages been waiting to hear? Let me linger over the answer. Consider the word we translate "secret" and which the Revised Standard Version translates "mystery." How does Paul use this word? In his commentary on Ephesians, Markus Barth says, "In Ephesians and Colossians the singular of the noun *mysterion* denotes an eternal decision of God which must now be proclaimed in the world."[3] In its nature the secret is not to be restricted to some inner circle of devotees or to religious professionals who are its guardians, but it is to be proclaimed throughout the world, to be shouted from the housetops. The time is at hand and the secret must be told.

Again, what is the secret? According to Barth, "Eph. 3:4 as much as says, this secret consists of the Messiah. His place with the Father, his commission, his coming, his death, his preaching, his work, his exaltation, and his headship over the church, the world, the powers, and all things."[4]

Paul makes an enormous claim, here and throughout his writings, that God has chosen to become known in human history, in human time and human life through Jesus of Nazareth, God's unique Son, the Messiah long promised in Old Testament scripture. This is the secret, its center and circumference, its heart and soul: Jesus, who is the Christ. The implications are vast, and Paul works with one of those implications in this passage—the implication that God loves the world, not just the Jewish race. Jesus Christ is universal, sent for Jew and Gentile alike. What is the secret? A universal Christ who is the Savior of the world. Paul commits himself, all the powers of mind and emotion, to make this secret known.

Responsive to Christ's Command

Christ's command is received by Paul at his conversion. The risen Christ says, "I have appeared to you for this purpose, to appoint you to serve and bear witness to . . . the Gentiles . . . to open their eyes, that they may turn from darkness to light" (Acts 26:16-18).

This is not as simple as it may sound to us, for it requires Paul to move against everything he knows and feels about the Gentile world as a first–century Jew. Who are the Gentiles? Romans who hold Israel in bondage, Greeks who worship idols, the Mediterranean world that seems to care for nothing but sensuality and violence. In Jesus' day and in Paul's day, the whole broad conservative wing of Judaism prays for and plans for the destruction of the Gentiles, looking for the angels of God to join them in a final conflict that would end Gentile domination forever. While Paul proclaims God's love in Christ for the Gentile world, contemporary Jews are writing *The War of the Sons of Light with the Sons of Darkness:*

> Lay thy hand on the necks of thy enemies
> and thy foot on the heaps of the slain;
> smite the nations, thy adversaries,
> and let thy sword consume guilty flesh.[5]

"The nations" are the Gentile nations. After all, they have done it to the Jews and to each other. And did not scripture provide ample warrant? "For the nation and kingdom that will not serve you shall perish; those nations shall be utterly laid waste" (Isa. 60:12). In their bondage to Rome and their history of Gentile oppression, it is far easier for this kind of passage to fire the national consciousness than it is for a passage like this: "I will give you as a light to the nations, that my salvation may reach to the ends of the earth" (Isa. 49:6).

What courage on the part of Paul; what breadth of spirit to move against the deeply-ingrained national hatred of Gentiles. And what a struggle to preach and teach that Gentiles are to share equally in the inheritance of Israel. It requires from Paul and every Jew who hears his message a radical change of heart. God's love is for all; the Messiah is universal.

Nor is this struggle simply among those outside the Christian community. Conflict arises between Peter and Paul. Peter, the most notable of the apostles, is the recognized leader of the rising church. It is Peter and other leaders of the Apostolic Council at Jerusalem who send Paul and Silas, and later Paul and Barnabas, to the Jewish communities in Asia Minor to tell the story of Jesus. As it happens, it is the Gentiles who respond more readily so that churches take root, grow, prosper, and multiply. Paul recognizes that God is calling Gentiles to faith in the Messiah and reports this to Peter and the council. The New Testament bears witness to the consternation this causes the Jewish Christians; but to make a long story short, the question is settled. The Christian story is for everyone. By the time the Gospel of John is written, perhaps 90 A.D., this is taken for granted. John writes, "For God so loved the world, that he gave his only begotten Son, that whosoever believeth in him should not perish, but have everlasting life" (John 3:16, KJV).

Paul discovers and proclaims what the church has since known through the centuries: the appeal of Jesus is universal. On my library shelf are several books of Christian art. One artist portrays Jesus as an African native; another pictures the child Jesus with the features and dress of an Oriental. A third paints a powerful scene of Jesus at prayer in Gethsemane as a Native American. There is a towering statue of Jesus on a ridge of the Andes Mountains that separates Chile and Argentina, though Jesus was born on the other side of the world. I remember an Eskimo woman I knew in Alaska who, tribal tattoos still on her face, would stand and in her own dialect tell of the Christ who had filled her heart with new life. No other leader has exerted so powerful an appeal or won such passionate devotion in every race. Buddha is Indian, Confucius is Chinese, Muhammad is Arabic, but Jesus Christ is universal.

What is there about him that is so magnetic? Back in the early 1900s, Charles Jefferson wrote, "Jesus changed men. He changed their habits and opinions and ambitions, he changed their tempers and dispositions and natures. He changed their hearts. They were never the same after they gave themselves up to him. . . . Wherever he went he transformed human lives."[6]

If we were to sort through a thousand paragraphs like the one above, if we were to read the hundreds of "lives of Jesus" that have been written, if we were to distill the message of the Gospels and the letters of the New Testament, what would lie at the heart of the Jesus story? What would be the essential kernel of truth? Just this: that God loves the world and sent Jesus to die for each of us and all of us. In Christ's resurrection God overcomes the power of death and promises us eternal life. This is the Christian story, the story of the universal Christ. What we do with it becomes our story.

Notes

1. Henry Snyder Gehman, ed., *New Westminster Dictionary of the Bible* (Philadelphia: Westminster Press, 1970), p. 53.
2. Amos Wilder, *Theopoetic* (Philadelphia: Fortress Press, 1976), p. 75.
3. Markus Barth, p. 329.
4. Ibid., p. 331.
5. Millar Burrows, *The Dead Sea Scrolls* (New York: The Viking Press, 1955), p. 398.
6. Charles E. Jefferson, *The Character of Jesus* (New York: Thomas Y. Crowell & Co., 1908), p. 348.

9. The Mediating Christ

3:7-13

There he kneels in the dark garden, arms stretched out before him on top of a rock, face lifted in prayer and illuminated by the light of God. Thorn bush in the foreground, sleeping disciples in the background, this painting, "Christ in Gethsemane," is one of the most widely known and best loved paintings in the world. The mood is intercession; on this last night of his life, Jesus labors in prayer over the path to Calvary and over all who would believe in his name. John records him praying, "I do not pray for these [the sleeping disciples] only, but also for those who believe in me through their word, that they may all be one; even as thou, Father, art in me, and I in thee, that they also may be in us, so that the world may believe that thou hast sent me" (John 17:20-21).

Surely this is one of the most dramatic prayers in scripture and one of the most memorable scenes. Judas has betrayed Jesus for thirty pieces of silver and soon will bestow upon him the traitor's kiss. Even now armed soldiers make their way toward the garden, and, as the last concern before the ordeal to come, Jesus prays for present and future disciples.

If people have only the most rudimentary knowledge about Jesus Christ, still they will understand that he has done something for all of us that opens the way to God. It is *for us* that he was born, lived, died, and was resurrected. This is basic, indissolubly bound to the gospel. Jesus is, as the title of the present chapter states, the mediating Christ.

In order to explore this at greater depth I chose two words from the text, ministry and mystery, and add a third word, mediation.

Ministry

Paul believes and states that he has received the gospel as a ministry. He writes, "Of this gospel I was made a minister according to the gift of God's grace which was given me by the working of his power."

Ministry: When you hear that word, what does it mean to you? It is one of the most common words in the Christian vocabulary, and therefore, like other overworked words, loses its force. Ordinarily we mean the professional ministry when we use it, that group of ordained persons who prefix their names with "Reverend." Or else we mean the visible program of a local congregation. The word comes to be our way of identifying the institutional church, its ordained leaders and its organized activity. That visible church is the one so easily held up to public caricature. We never said we were perfect, and there is no lack of those wanting to remind us of our imperfection. Sometimes those committed to the church get a little angry, other times they just grin and bear it. How can you help but smile when you read this old notice originally published in Great Britain at the beginning of World War II: "All persons in the above age groups are required to register for national service except lunatics, the blind, and ministers of religion." [1]

When we are all done criticizing our clergy, who are just as human as anyone else, and when we are done with caricatures of the church, we have not exhausted the word *ministry.* Something far more dynamic lies within it. Let me try to trace it out. The word goes back to a Latin root that means "to serve." And that word, *minister,* is a translation of the Greek word Paul uses, *diakonos,* from which we get our English word *deacon.* Ministry is service, no more and no less, and a minister is one who serves. But how ordinary that sentence sounds, how expected and conventional, and therefore how dull! What are we missing then, what are we overlooking that the words *ministry* and *service* should be so flat and indistinct? Let me suggest that the church has trivialized the words by confining Christian service to institutional maintenance. Yes, somebody has got to take up the offering and polish the church silver, but we impoverish the word unless we identify ourselves as disciples of the Christ who "came not to be served but to serve, and to give his life as a ransom for many" (Matt. 20:28). "Ministry" does not come to life for us until we extend ourselves, spend ourselves, and give ourselves to others for Jesus' sake.

Henri Nouwen writes helpfully on this theme:

> Ministry means the ongoing attempt to put one's own search for God, with all the moments of pain and joy, despair and hope, at the disposal of those who want to join this search but do not know how. Therefore, ministry in no way is a privilege. Instead, it is the core of the Christian life. No Christian is a Christian without being a minister. . . . But whatever form the Christian ministry

takes, the basis is always the same: to lay down one's life for one's friends.[2]

We will continue to yawn when we hear the word *ministry* until we know and experience the power resident within it. Where does this ministry of which Paul speaks come from? Not from him! It is a gift he has received, a grace that has penetrated to the depths of his life, beginning in his unsought and unmerited vision of Christ on the Damascus Road. Listen to him talk about it: "Of this gospel I was made a minister according to the gift of God's grace which was given me by the working of his power." The language of this text is energy language. The mood is active and not passive. One feels within it a flow of grace abounding, of life-changing spiritual power. Paul's whole world has been turned upside down by Jesus Christ, and he is convinced the same thing will happen to those whose mortal lives are also touched by God in Jesus Christ. To be in ministry is to be an agent of this transforming grace.

Paul's heart is on his sleeve as he writes this passage. He almost bends over backward to make his point that the gospel is God's gift and comes from nothing in himself. How pointed the contrast he draws: "To me, though I am the very least of all the saints, this grace was given, to preach to the Gentiles the unsearchable riches of Christ." In more contemporary words, Paul is saying something like this: "Even though I persecuted the church and tried to destroy it, being an enemy of Christ, still in love he revealed himself to me, forgave me, and wonder of wonders, made me a minister in the very church I had sought to destroy. I was intending death to followers of Jesus, but he has given me life!"

What lies behind Paul's words? Nothing less than the

center of the gospel message: that Jesus has given himself for us without reserve, laying down his life sacrificially. He has done it in obedience to the will of God in order to open a way to God for us. When we were hiding out from God like Adam and Eve, when we were blinded to God by our own self-concern, when we rejected or neglected anything that had to do with the spiritual world, "while we were yet sinners Christ died for us" (Rom. 5:8). When people make a connection with the God who loves us and seeks us in Jesus Christ, feeling the claim of that love, they begin to know the motivation within ministry. John puts it simply, "We love, because he first loved us" (1 John 4:19).

One more idea: Jesus said in John 15:13, "Greater love has no man than this, that a man lay down his life for his friends." Henri Nouwen speaks to this verse: "Why does a man lay down his life for his friends? There is only one answer to that question: to give new life. All functions of the ministry are life giving. "[3]

Mystery

Paul says that he has been called to preach "the unsearchable riches of Christ," so that all might see "what is the plan of the mystery hidden for ages in God who created all things."

Biblical scholars have spent lifetimes examining the books of the Bible in the greatest detail using all the tools of scholarship available. Archaeologists have sifted through the sands of Israel holding a Bible in one hand and asking to what extent the record in stone and clay bears out the biblical record. Historians, sociologists, professors of world religion, and psychologists have all applied their disciplines in examining the Bible and weighing its authority. No other book has been the object of such concentrated attention from experts. The temptation is to reduce the Bible to sociology, history, or literature; to comprehend and categorize it as one more natural phenomenon. This leaves the scholar in control and the rational mind the final judge of scripture and God.

Yet, one reading of a passage like Ephesians 3:7-13 poses an additional realm of truth and an additional method of approach. When Paul speaks of "the unsearchable riches of Christ," when he declares that he was "made a minister according to the gift of God's grace," when he uses the words, "the plan of the mystery hidden for ages in God" and refers to God's "eternal purpose," then we know we are in a realm of truth not contradictory to but different than rational inquiry. It is a realm in which we use words like *revelation* and quote verses like Romans 11:33, "O the depth of the riches and wisdom and knowledge of God! How unsearchable are his judgments and how inscrutable his ways!" The Bible is a book bearing witness to the self-disclosure of God, a book revealing God in search of us. No matter how many degrees one may write after one's name or how wide one's experience in the world, one is still mortal, standing in the midst of fathomless mystery, often feeling like a motherless child lost in the vast abysses of space and time.

Once we allow ourselves to experience the wonder of it all, we stop the self-delusion that we are in control, knowing that we are creatures and letting our native impulses begin to pray, "O God, I need you!" Life devoid of mystery is a moonscape. And the god whom we can understand is always spelled with a small "g" and always an idol. To avoid any kind of obscurantism or false dividing of the world into physical and spiritual, we should say it again: God is not less than rational but more than rational. To believe in God is not to contradict the truth we learn in the natural world but to expand it.

When you repeat the creeds of the church as a part of worship, when you study the confessions of the church written across the centuries and see the libraries of books on Christian theology, you are tempted to believe Christianity is constructed of intellectual formulations. But back of all this writing and study is something else that produced it and motivated the authors, and that something is the indefinable touch of the spirit of God on the human spirit. It is a thing of mystery which, like love, poetry, prayer, and music, will not fit neatly into rational categories but belongs to the realm of mystery. Surely G.K. Chesterton was thinking about this when he wrote:

> This world is wild as an old wives' tale,
> And strange the plain things are,
> The earth is enough and the air is enough
> For our wonder and our war;
> But our rest is as far as the fire-drake swings
> And our peace is put in impossible things
> Where clashed and thundered unthinkable wings
> Round an incredible star.[4]

Mediation

One of the ways to discover the meaning in a particular passage of scripture is to ask whether there is a central idea around which the passage gathers or toward which the passage moves. In Ephesians 3:7-13, access to God is the focus. Reducing the verses to their essence would yield a sentence like this: "The gospel of which Paul is a minister is the unfathomable mystery revealed through the church that all have access to God through Jesus Christ."

What is the part played by Jesus? He is the mediator, the one standing between a lost and fallen humanity and a holy God who is both just and loving. There is a gulf that must be bridged, a barrier that must be removed, a resistance that must be overcome in order for men and women to find reconciliation and peace with God. The image that fits the word *access* is that of someone leading another into the presence of a ruler or king. To have access is to be granted the privilege of admission to the presence of the king. It is Jesus who holds us with one hand and God with the other, uniting us with the God who is Mother, Father, Source, and Ground of our lives. Though we were separated from God by our sins, we are united with God by what Jesus has done on our behalf. He is the mediating Christ.

New Testament verses speak of this in different ways: "Christ also died for sins once for all, the righteous for the unrighteous, that he might bring us to God" (1 Pet. 3:18); "Christ has entered, not a sanctuary made with hands, a copy of the true one, but into heaven itself, now to appear in the presence of God on our behalf" (Heb. 9:24).

What we cannot do for ourselves, what we can neither merit nor deserve, Jesus does for us. It is the grace of God. How treasured in Christian devotion through the centuries has been the Christ pleading our cause before God, winning for us God's acceptance, opening up the kingdom of God that we might have hope for all the years to come. There is exhilaration in the way Paul describes our coming into the presence of God. We come with a free and singing spirit, with a boldness permeated by joy, a gladness of heart beyond words to tell.

It is easy for Christians to overlook the age-old agonizing search for God that has marked the human journey across time. The lament of Job, "Oh, that I knew where I might find him, that I might come even to his seat" (23:3), has been the lament of humankind. It is a hunger that lies at the very root of our being. To be released from the burden of my sins, to provide an answer for the inevitability of my death, to give voice to the spiritual core within me all make clear our hunger for God.

A number of years ago a plane carrying a rugby team from Uruguay crashed in the Andes Mountains. Only sixteen of the original forty-five crew and passengers survived ten weeks of bitter cold. After waiting at the wreck for some two months, two young men decided to try walking out. Ten days later these men, Parrado and Canessa, made their first contact with the outside world, seeing a Chilean horseman across a torrential mountain stream. They shouted, but he didn't hear. In desperation they fell to their knees and raised their hands in prayer. When he finally saw them, he wrote out a message on a piece of paper, tied it to a stone and threw it across the stream. It read, "There is a man coming later. . . . tell me what you want." They wrote a reply and threw it back. He signaled that he understood. Then he took a piece of bread out of his pocket, threw it to them, and waved as he climbed down out of view. They held the bread in their hands, this tangible sign that they had contacted the outside world. Canessa turned to his friend, and looking at the bread, cried, "We're saved!" "Yes," replied Parrado, "we're saved."[5]

Christians have made the discovery that God's eternal kingdom, God's life and love are found in the mediating Christ. We, too, are saved.

Notes

1. Robert McAfee Brown, *The Significance of the Church* (Philadelphia: Westminster Press, 1956), p. 84.
2. Henri Nouwen, *Creative Ministry* (New York: Doubleday & Company, Image Books, 1978), p. 114.
3. Ibid., pp. 114-5.
4. Gilbert K. Chesterton, "The House of Christians," in *Collected Poems* (New York: Dodd, Mead & Company, 1932), p. 130.
5. Piers Paul Read, *Alive* (Philadelphia: J.B. Lippencott Company, 1974), p. 272.

10. The Indwelling Christ
3:14-21

I can remember sitting in my mother's lap to hear a story. Maybe you can too. Though it was a long time ago, I can recall the pleasure this gave me and how much I anticipated the story hour. "Peter Rabbit," "The Three Bears," "Jack and the Beanstalk," "Hansel and Gretel"—these and other stories helped to form my childhood.

There were also family stories: My grandfather who had traveled around the world and could "spin a yarn" about Australia's outback; my English grandmother who read tea leaves and told of seeing a disembodied spirit in her childhood home; my handsome uncle who rode motorcycles in the twenties; the annual fermentation of the elderberry wine; the loss of the family farm in the Great Depression. These and other stories belong to our family and help to tell us who we are.

Stories are far older than writing. Ancient people remembered their history in story form. Today we call it "oral history." These people told their tribal stories around campfires, remembering the deeds and discoveries of their ancestors—how the tribe first got horses, the severity of a particular winter, battle exploits of a great chief. Long after writing had been refined, stories continued to be a part of life. For example, rhapsodes or storytellers recited the entire *Iliad* of Homer by memory as a part of the Olympic Games in ancient Greece. This is how people knew themselves and who they were.

The Bible is the storybook of our Christian faith. It contains a broad range of literature: poetry like the Psalms, wisdom literature like the Proverbs, history like Kings and Chronicles, prophecy like Isaiah and Amos, apocalyptic writing like Revelation, the New Testament letters, the passionate witness of the Gospels to Jesus Christ. All these types or genres of literature, written over so many centuries of time, unite around a central theme: encounter and relationship with God. These writers bear solemn testimony that they know God, that God is part of their personal and corporate lives, and that God enters and shapes their historical experience. They speak of the covenant they make with the God whom they worship and tell us we can be partners in the same covenant: "Yes, you are our God! Yes, we are your people!"

There is great literature in the Bible. There are enlightening historical materials, memorable stories, moral and spiritual insights, but none of these things explains our lasting fascination with the book and its power in our lives. What is its secret? It is a story about human beings like ourselves who met and knew God, human beings indelibly marked by hope and fear, mortality, selfishness and savageness, pain, great questions, love and loyalty, weakness and betrayal, hunger for God. In some uncanny and unpredictable way, when we fallible, sinful humans read this Bible, when we hear it preached and taught, we feel the breath of God. Because it speaks to our humanity so unerringly, it is a universal book.

Why introduce this chapter by talking about the place

of story in our lives? Because our familiarity with the biblical story can anesthetize us to its meaning. We have heard it all so many times before that its grandeur fades the way the grandeur of a mountain skyline can fade when we see it every day. We choose a text, Ephesians 3:14-21, and a chapter title, "The Indwelling Christ," and it all sounds so comfortable, so predictable in a biblical commentary. But behind the title is an immense claim. The infinite universe above our heads is not empty but is an expression of a Creator whose will has brought it into being and whose power sustains it. It is not a chance occurrence in a void. It is not finally subject to the dominion of death. The last word has not been spoken when science has enunciated its laws of matter and motion. The world is full of mystery and keeps on pointing beyond itself. And in the midst of it all, we human beings keep on having undeniable experience of God. The Bible is a book that bears witness to this experience throughout its pages. Our text is but one example of a continuing story. There seem to be two ways we sense and know God: As distant and as near. To use bigger words, we feel the transcendence and the immanence of God. The Bible reflects the majesty and the friendship of God, the wonder and the welcome of God. This chapter wants to look carefully at both kinds of experience.

The Distance of God

Paul writes, "For this reason I bow my knees before the Father, from whom every family in heaven and on earth is named, . . . according to the riches of his glory." The translation "I bow my knees before the Father" is less than adequate because Paul uses a word that means "to spread oneself out face down before God," perhaps like a monk in his cell lying face down in prayer in the form of a cross. When the text speaks of "the riches of his glory," it ushers us into the majestic presence of God. That presence is identified in scripture by radiance, by a light so intense that no human eye can gaze upon it. It is this brilliance which makes the biblical writers say things like, "Let us offer to God acceptable worship, with reverence and awe; for our God is a consuming fire" (Heb. 12:28-29) and, "Out of Zion, the perfection of beauty, God shines forth" (Psalm 50:2). Second Chronicles records that when the temple of Solomon was dedicated it was filled with such light that the priests could no longer perform their duties. "The glory of the Lord filled the house of God" (5:14).

One has to ask whether the contemporary church is in touch with the majesty of God and to what extent it shapes our life and worship. Surely contemporary theology is steering a wide course around this central theme of scripture. These irrepressible ascriptions of praise, these glad assertions about the majesty of God, these words of adoration rise up like incense from the ancient page. The Bible is crowded with such language: "To him who sits upon the throne . . . be blessing and honor and glory and might for ever and ever!" (Rev. 5:13); "Holy, holy, holy is the Lord of hosts; the whole earth is full of his glory" (Isa. 6:3). The people of the Bible sense the majesty of God, respond to the mystery of God, have an inner capacity for adoration. What about us? We are not exactly in the habit of holding our lives close to the holy flame. It seems so foreign to the way we think and speak. Maybe it has to do with a lifestyle too bound up with getting and spending. Maybe we are in such retreat from mystery, from things we cannot analyze and control, that we simply tune out. Not being able to face death, we talk about funeral arrangements. Not being able to face an unknown future, we think little beyond weekend plans or the next vacation. Not being able to face the meaning of allegiance to Jesus Christ, the Lord of life, we talk about church membership. Not being able to face the whole question of God, we simply give up church. And then, having avoided the deepest things in life, we wonder why our days grow stale, why we are bored, why everything seems repetitious and flat. This is true for us, I believe, to the extent that the life force of God, the very source of our being, has no central place within us. Soon the spiritual world seems only a distant rumor while the here and now demands more and more from us. We become like seeds within an orange, drawing our life from the orange, with its nature and character all through us, yet unaware of the orange or even denying its existence.

When Paul calls God "Father," he tells us that there is a divine love on which we can depend. When he says that "every family in heaven and on earth" receives its name from God, he tells us of God's universal dominion. And when he adds the phrase "riches of his glory," Paul draws on the biblical vision of the majesty of God. This is the Creator without beginning or end of days, the one who stands beyond the borders of time and who is the beginning and the end. This is the God whom the Latin church fathers called *mysterium tremendum,* the unfathomable mystery.

In using the word *distance* to describe one of the two ways the Bible talks about our experience of God, I hope to point to our inherent awe and wonder before God. It is a native impulse. Kenneth Grahame's book, *The Wind in the Willows,* makes the point superbly. There is a passage in which Rat and Mole are looking for Portly, a baby otter who had gotten lost. In the midst of their search, they hear the unearthly music of the "piper at the gates of dawn," the animal's god Pan. They make their way toward the source of the music.

> Then suddenly the Mole felt a great Awe fall upon him, an awe that turned his muscles to water, bowed his head, and rooted his feet to the ground. It was no panic terror—indeed he felt wonderfully at peace and happy—but it was an awe that smote and held him and, without seeing, he knew it could only mean that some august Presence was very, very near.

Grahame calls Pan "the friend and Helper," and there with him is the baby otter, safe and content. Mole is the first to speak.

> "Rat!" he found breath to whisper, shaking. "Are you afraid?"
>
> "Afraid?" murmured the Rat, his eyes shining with unutterable love. "Afraid! Of *Him?* O, never, never! And yet—and yet—O Mole, I am afraid." [1]

The Nearness of God

Like two strands woven to form a single cord, Paul weaves together the distance and the nearness of God. In prayer he prostrates himself before the God of glory whose presence "is a consuming fire," asking that the Ephesian believers may be strengthened at the core of life by the spirit of this eternal Father. And then, more specific still, more personal still, he prays that "Christ may dwell in your hearts through faith." Familiarity robs us of the startling impact of this verse. God has chosen to become known in Jesus of Nazareth as in no other. We

Christians believe that. We remember Peter saying on the Day of Pentecost, "Let all the house of Israel therefore know assuredly that God has made him both Lord and Christ, this Jesus whom you crucified" (Acts 2:36). We accept the witness of Colossians 1:15 that Jesus "is the image of the invisible God." We remember Jesus saying after the resurrection, "I am with you always, to the close of the age" (Matt. 28:20). But as much as we read these New Testament statements, and no matter how well we articulate a theology about the indwelling Christ, still we must keep alive to the wonder of it, keep our hearts tender to the intimacy of it, keep our minds open to the mystery of it. In some way that eludes our words, Christ dwells within. His spirit engages our human spirits. How? One can only mix images in response. He makes the inner life burn with a finer fire, tunes our whole being to a sweeter harmony, breathes a fragrance of love and hope, pushes back our darkness, so that we find freedom to become what God calls us to be and to do what God calls us to do in our world. Nor is this indwelling of Christ temporary or occasional. The word itself indicates permanent residence. Just as the high point of Paul's teaching about the church is the dwelling of God in the holy temple built of living stones, so the high point of Paul's teaching about individual Christians is the dwelling of Christ within each.

One more comment on the nearness of God in Jesus Christ: The glory always identified with the presence of God has already been a topic of contemplation, but I want to carry it a step further. That divine presence touched the life of Israel in the pillar of fire and the pillar of cloud that led the way through the wilderness, in the cloud that covered Sinai when Moses was on its smoking summit receiving the Commandments, and in the cloud that filled Solomon's temple at its dedication. In the New Testament that same cloud of glory reappeared with Jesus on the Mount of Transfiguration (Mark 9:2-8). In fact Jesus himself is identified by New Testament writers as the glory of God present in the world:

> He reflects the glory of God and bears the very stamp of his nature.
>
> —Hebrews 1:3

> And the Word became flesh and dwelt among us, full of grace and truth; we have beheld his glory, glory as of the only Son from the Father.
>
> —John 1:14

> For it is the God who said, "Let light shine out of darkness," who has shone in our hearts to give the light of the knowledge of the glory of God in the face of Christ.
>
> —2 Corinthians 4:6

What more needs to be said? The indwelling Christ present with us in our life's journey will be present with us at the river of death. This Companion, Guide, and Morning Star is the presence of God with us and our hope for all the years to come.

It is on the basis of this revelation of God to us and within us that Paul extends his prayer to ask that we, "being rooted and grounded in love, may have power to comprehend with all the saints what is the breadth and length and height and depth, and to know the love of Christ which surpasses knowledge." In this prayer Paul makes an urgent plea that the Ephesian church dig its spiritual foundations deep, and then, changing images in mid-sentence, he urges that the church root its life in the nourishing soil of the love of Christ. Only so, he may be thinking, will the church have power to proclaim its message. Only so will it make an impact on its world.

The Revised Standard Version gives the translation of verse 18 already quoted, "power to comprehend with all the saints." Because of the nature of the verb, a better translation would be "be strong to grasp," or "to lay hold on." The laying hold on faith and its growth within us is inevitably "with all the saints," as Paul says. The Bible knows nothing of solitary religion. It is in the womb of the church that our spiritual birth occurs and in the bosom of the church that we are nourished in the life of the spirit. It is in the fellowship and teaching of the church that we grow to maturity. With whom? With our sisters and brothers sharing a journey of faith, "with all the saints." One of the deep and abiding joys of Christianity is the love we discover for each other in our mutual love for Jesus Christ. It is a unity that can bridge all the other divisions that would make us enemies or strangers.

To conclude, scripture is filled with images of the nearness of God. The Old Testament pictures it in the intimate image of Israel as the wife Yahweh tenderly loves but who is unfaithful (Ezek. 16). The psalmist speaks of the distance of God, who is "a great King above all gods," and the nearness of God: "For he is our God, and we are the people of his pasture, and the sheep of his hand" (95:3, 7).

The Bible, our innate desire to worship, our human need, Christianity itself—all are calling us to hold in balance these two sides of our experience of God—distance and nearness, majesty and familiarity, wonder and welcome. The Creator is the loving Father. The majestic God is humbled so that we may see the divine face in Jesus Christ. Appropriately enough, this passage ends with an ascription of praise, rising irrepressibly from one whose heart has been won by an indwelling Christ: "Now to him who by the power at work within us is able to do far more abundantly than all that we ask or think, to him be glory in the church and in the Christ Jesus to all generations, for ever and ever. Amen."

Notes

1. Kenneth Grahame, *The Wind in the Willows* (New York: Charles Scribner's Sons, 1933, reprinted 1961), pp. 134-5, 136.

IV

SENT FOR THE CHURCH

11. *The Source of Unity*

4:1-6

Chapter 4 begins the second major section of the letter to the Ephesians. The division of the letter could not be more pronounced. Chapters 1-3 are major teaching chapters written in the mood of praise to God for the gift of Jesus Christ and for the place of the church in the design of God. Chapters 4-6 are chapters on Christian living, beginning with the sentence, "I, therefore, a prisoner of the Lord, beg you to lead a life worthy of the calling to which you have been called."

It has often been said that when you see a *therefore* in scripture, ask what it is there for. This particular *therefore* is a significant one, bearing the weight of the three preceding chapters. Paul is saying, in effect, "In the light of all I have written up to this point, and in the light of God's gracious self-giving in Jesus Christ, to whom I am bound in obedient service, I beg you to live out the truth of your calling."

Paul has already made abundantly clear the disunity and disharmony of the world. People are divided within themselves at the very core of life and therefore are distant from God. The effect of this spiritual alienation is visible in the division between nations, races, and religions. The one great hope of the world for unity is the Christ whom God has sent, through whom God's purposes must triumph. And the one vehicle God has chosen to be the instrument of those purposes is the church. If unity is not a resident reality in the church, not a native expression of the life of the church, then God's purposes are frustrated. To see this is to understand the critical importance of Paul's opening exhortation: "I. . . beg you to lead a life worthy of the calling to which you have been called." God's grand design of bringing unity and harmony to the world is a design dependent on the harmony and unity of the church.

In the two sentences of Ephesians 4:1-6, Paul covers a lot of ground, focusing on unity in three ways: unity within oneself, unity within the local congregation, and unity within the whole church. The importance of each of these spheres of unity deserves individual treatment.

Unity Within Oneself

Paul says, "Lead a life worthy of the calling." What calling? The call of God in Jesus Christ to which the Ephesians have responded individually; the appeal of the gospel that has sounded within each person leading to repentance and faith; the affirmation of each that Jesus is Lord and consequent membership in the company of believers—that calling! Since this calling must be owned by each individual, Paul encourages each to a unity of life and word. "Live out your calling as a follower of Jesus"—this is the exhortation.

The problem that gives rise to Paul's appeal is the lack of harmony between what Christians say and do. To quote an old spiritual, "Ev'rybody talkin' 'bout-a Heaven ain-a goin' there." And to quote a sermonic line I have heard a hundred times, "Some people are talkin' the talk without walkin' the walk." As a matter of fact, that's the word the King James Version uses: "I . . . beseech you that ye walk worthy of the vocation wherewith ye are called."

What is the flavor of this verb *walk*? Barth's commentary replies, "In Pauline Letters the Greek verb 'to walk' . . . suggests something different from a casual promenade: it means to follow a prescribed way in a fixed order, comparable to the march of Israel under God's guidance in the wilderness."[1]

Behind Paul's urgent appeal to Ephesian believers are these concerns: our lack of coherence as Christian human beings, our vacillation between secular and Christian lifestyles, our slowness in growing into the image of Christ, and therefore our clouded witness in the world. Paul speaks in the imperative mode: "Lead a life worthy of your calling!" That is, let the honor of that calling inspire you, let the author of that calling strengthen you, let the wonder of that calling shape your vision of who you are—a child of God through Jesus Christ.

Paul can hear the questions coming: "But tell me what to do! What are the specifics? How shall I live a worthy life?" Yet, he gives no easy answers that can be handed out like business cards. Rather than a list of prohibitions, he gives a catalog of broad-based virtues, the very atmosphere of the life in Christ: lowliness, meekness, and patience. As these virtues are assimilated into the character of those who love Jesus, these believers will live lives worthy of their calling. Each of these virtues is worth comment.

Lowliness: The more common translation of this word is "humility," and it was seen not as a virtue but as a character defect in the non-Christian world of Paul's day.

It carried the connotation of weakness and servility. The Greek or Roman would choose great-heartedness as one of the pillars of a noble character, but never lowliness. Christians, of course, chose this term because of Jesus, who, in Paul's words, "made himself of no reputation, and took upon him the form of a servant" (Phil. 2:7, KJV). One of the classic references for humility is Matthew 23:12, where Jesus tells his disciples and the scribes and Pharisees, "Whoever exalts himself will be humbled, and whoever humbles himself will be exalted." To be humble is to be honest about who we are, to be able to see our own weakness and self-absorption. To be humble is to measure the success of our own character and calling by the life of Christ. To define humility like this is to accept it as the ground of all the virtues, the rich soil in which the seeds of Christian character can take root and grow.

Meekness: Just to read the word is to recognize the resistance it creates in us. It calls up images of the old cartoon character Caspar Milquetoast, who, upon reading a highway sign saying, "Danger, Falling Rocks," turns the car around and goes home. In a contemporary American culture captivated by violence, meekness is despised. We need a different translation, perhaps "gentleness." This means more than mild, though still it will be greeted with reluctance by a great many Christians. We don't want to hear the church defined as "a group of mild-mannered people being lectured to be more mild-mannered by a mild-mannered preacher." Why, then, is this a definitive trait of Christian character? Because it is a Christ-like virtue. Jesus is born in the humblest of circumstances and takes up his ministry among the socially despised, the sick and troubled, announcing, "The Spirit of the Lord is upon me, because he has anointed me to preach good news to the poor" (Luke

4:18). He does not seek to establish himself at the centers of political power; he opposes physical violence and submits to humiliation and death at the hands of Roman authority. He is a man of gentleness, yet in that gentleness is a strength far greater than military might or political power, a strength that lifts empires off their hinges and profoundly alters the course of human civilization. To be a disciple of Jesus is to see the deeper meanings that lie within gentleness and is therefore to comprehend T.S. Eliot's line:

> In the juvescence of the year
> came Christ the tiger.[2]

Patience: Many people hear the word *patience* impatiently. Maybe they heard a thousand times from a parent, a teacher, a boss, or a spouse, "Just be patient!" They felt pushed aside. Or, as McNeill, Morrison, and Nouwen suggest, the counsel of patience can be manipulative, "used by the powerful to keep the powerless under control."[3] But the counsel toward patience in our text is positive, listing patience as an essential ingredient in Christian character. No doubt the term will elicit less than enthusiastic response in us until we see patience as an inseparable part of the love of God. God is patient with us. Second Peter puts it this way: "The Lord is . . . forbearing toward you, not wishing that any should perish" (3:9). *Patience, forbearance, longsuffering* are English versions of the same Greek word. God gives space; God makes room for grace to bear fruit in our lives. It follows that we who have experienced this kind of generosity will, in gratitude, exhibit the same patience toward others. When the going gets tough, when people get angry, when accusations fly, when others don't carry through, the Christian spirit is steady, does not blame, can absorb criticism without retaliation, and is not defeated or bitter because "love is patient and kind. . . . It is not irritable or resentful. . . . Love bears all things, believes all things, hopes all things, endures all things" (2 Cor. 13:4-5,7). Patience is not a passive enduring of wrong but a positive witness to God's love in Jesus Christ and to the ultimate truth of God's kingdom.

In sum, the Christian leads a life worthy of God's call when there is unity of life and word. That unity is shaped and perfected as the lowliness, meekness, and patient love of Christ are assimilated into Christian character.

Unity Within the Local Congregation

One need not have wide experience in churches in order to realize the lack of unity in the local congregation. The New Testament letters and church history in general bear ample witness to disunity, a continuing struggle across the generations. During the Great Awakening, for example,

> A Connecticut layman . . . grew angry over what he judged to be the doctrinal deviations of his minister. At length he took his ax to the meetinghouse, chopped out the entire pew in which he and his family had worshipped since the church was built, and took it home to his attic. The pew became the symbolic center for other dissenting members, who soon formed a new church of their own.[4]

When Paul talks about "forbearing one another in love," he is appealing to Ephesian Christians for unity in the local congregation. The love of Christ that believers are internalizing, the traits of Christian character being formed in them are not simply for a rehearsal of private virtue, but for strengthening the Christian community. Paul's urgent exhortation makes clear that this is of the highest importance. If unity is not the prevailing mood of the church, then how will the church be able to demonstrate the unity God offers the world in Jesus Christ? Be "eager to maintain the unity of the Spirit in the bond of peace," he writes. "Get with it! Don't delay! Pursue it! Go ahead and do it! Don't waste any time, either!" This is the tone of his language. *The New English Bible* translates the phrase, "Spare no effort."

Paul is not urging the Ephesians to *attain* the unity of the Spirit, but to *maintain* the unity of the Spirit. Since there is no authentic Christian community without the Spirit, they are to be sensitive to that which is already in their midst: the Spirit's unifying presence. It is as if unity is a reality that can be driven out by strife, blame, spiritual one-upsmanship, and other forms of behavior that are contrary to lowliness, meekness, and patient love.

But what is the nature of the unity that Paul urges? Obviously it does not mean uniformity, a kind of ecclesiastical "same-speak," for difference is essential to a living church. "We though many" is Paul's way of talking about unity (Rom. 12:5). Neither is unity an absence of disagreement. Looking at something from differing perspectives is a path to truth, and we in the church owe brothers and sisters in faith our honest opinion over the issues we discuss. Honestly considering two or more sides of a question is essential to our growth and maturity as human beings both in the church and out of it, for any relationship that is interpersonal inevitably uncovers points of disagreement. The question then becomes one of loving consideration for my Christian brother or sister in the disagreement we experience. After all, I can disagree with you without pouring a cup of hot soup in your lap. Jitsuo Morikawa hit the nail on the head when he said in a sermon at Riverside Church in New York City, "The great strength and weakness of Riverside today lies in its disputing diversity, so that we wonder whether its contrasts . . . will shatter this church or become the source of creative tension, finding outlet in a new burst of surprising energy."[5]

Some of us may hope we don't walk that close to the edge of disaster, but disagreement is inescapable in the church and energy producing as long as we "maintain the unity of the Spirit." Do we care enough to disagree? Are we well enough informed to disagree or do we just fight? Do we love each other enough to disagree without breaking fellowship?

Given the imperfection of Christian character most of us demonstrate and knowing what churches are like, it is helpful to realize that unity is not the perfection of fellowship. It is a gift because we actually do discover that Christ breaks down barriers that separate us from each other, but it is also a goal and a task because that unity is so imperfect. Yes, the gift is ours, but in our humanness we depend on the formative power of the Holy Spirit to heal the divisions that still separate us from others who give allegiance to the same Christ.

Unity Within the Whole Church

Verses 4-6 read like a poetic confession of faith used in worship or a catechism used in teaching. The form is trinitarian, using Spirit, Lord (Jesus Christ), and God the Father. Paul is anxious to give theological weight to the appeal for unity. It follows that if God is one, then the world that is created by God and related to God must be one as well. Unity, then, is not merely the emotional need of the Christian community but the necessary implication of God's dominion and care of all the world. After all, God is in the business of bringing order out of chaos. The story of the Tower of Babel in Genesis 11 explains how humankind, once unified in language and common life, became scattered and divided. The root evils of pride and arrogance have destroyed the original unity. It is not by chance that Genesis 12 follows with the story of Abram and Sarai, whom God called to be the first parents of a new people, a people one in faith and obedience to the one God.

As the Old Testament begins to unfold, we see visible signs of the unity of Israel, the people of God. They share the dramatic experience of deliverance from bondage in Egypt. At God's initiative they affirm a covenant of mutual faithfulness: God says, "I will be your God," and they respond, "We will be your people." This covenant is sealed in the giving of the law at Sinai as Israel pledges obedience to God's will. Eventually they become established in "the promised land." Still later they build the Temple at Jerusalem. All these things are powerful symbols of unity: deliverance, covenant, law, land, and Temple.

But succeeding generations reveal Israel's struggle to maintain unity and her frequent failure. She breaks covenant by worshiping the gods of surrounding nations; the unified kingdom so glorious under King David is divided by internal strife and periodic civil war follows; eventually the Temple itself is destroyed, and the land is conquered by Gentile nations. Reading these stories today does not begin to make clear to us the tragedy for Israel. Who were they without land or temple? What about the promise of Abraham? Where was God?

It is against the background of Israel's painful history that Paul writes. God has not forsaken these people but has been working out the divine purposes from generation to generation, preparing the world for the coming of the Christ. This Christ stands at the center of God's grand design. In him all things come to consummation; in him all broken lines converge; in him all God's purposes are fulfilled and all the world reconciled in justice and love. Paul's words rise and soar as he writes, "There is one body and one Spirit, just as you were called to the one hope that belongs to your call, one Lord, one faith, one baptism, one God and Father of us all." If, as Teilhard de Chardin writes, there is an "irresistible instinct in our hearts which leads us toward unity,"[6] then here is the vision of a harmony as wide as the whole creation. As time moves forward toward the final kingdom, God's arms are wrapped around the world, encircling it in a saving purpose in Christ so that all people joined to him in loving trust will be united with each other. There can be no mistaking that Christ is the unifying center. The closer women and men come to him, the closer they will come to each other. To say it another way, in the New Testament unity is inevitably Christological. The source of unity is Christ. As Adam was representative of the whole human race, so Jesus Christ is representative of a new humanity.

Alas, the visible church seems to be about a light year away from this crystal vision. So was the New Testament church! Yet, as Ernst Kasemann observes, "In spite of all its vicissitudes, its tensions and its contradictions, primitive Christianity proclaimed the one Church, not in the sense of a theory of organic development but in the name of the reality and the truth of the Holy Spirit."[7]

What are we to conclude? That the unity in Christ we

have experienced is real! We feel the power of Galatians 3:28, "There is neither Jew nor Greek, there is neither slave nor free, there is neither male nor female; for you are all one in Christ Jesus." And we feel the truth of Jesus' words, "I have other sheep, that are not of this fold; I must bring them also, and they will heed my voice. So there shall be one flock, one shepherd" (John 10:16). And it is enough for us to find our place in the beloved community of the church and to pray as we move forward, "Thy kingdom come, Thy will be done, On earth as it is in heaven."

Notes

1. Markus Barth, *Ephesians: Translation and Commentary on Chapters 4-6*, vol. 34A of *The Anchor Bible* (New York: Doubleday & Company, 1974), p. 427.
2. T. S. Eliot, "Gerontion," in *The Complete Poems and Plays, 1909-1950* (San Diego: Harcourt, Brace, Jovanovich, 1952), p. 21.
3. Donald McNeill, Douglas Morrison, and Henri Nouwen, *Compassion: A Reflection on the Christian Life* (New York: Doubleday & Company, 1982), p. 93.
4. Richard Hofstadter, *America at 1750* (New York: Alfred A. Knopf, 1971; New York: Random House, Vintage Books, 1973), p. 282.
5. Jitsuo Morikawa, "Anguish of the Ministry," a sermon delivered at Riverside Church, New York, 1 May 1977.
6. Pierre Teilhard de Chardin, p. 266.
7. Ernst Kasemann, *New Testament Questions of Today* (Philadelphia: Fortress Press, 1969), p. 257.

12. The Giver of Gifts

4:7-13

A letter was received at the post office of a small city addressed simply to God. It was obviously a child's handwriting. Not knowing what to do with it and unable to forward it, a postal employee opened it and read: "Dear God, my name is Jimmy. I am seven years old. My father is dead and my mother is having a hard time raising me and my sister. Could you send us five hundred dollars?" The postal worker showed the letter to some co-workers and they decided to kick in a few dollars each to send to the family. The total came to three hundred dollars. A couple of weeks later a second letter came addressed to God in the same handwriting. It was opened, and this is what it said: "Dear God, thank you very much for helping us. We really appreciate it. But the next time would you please leave the money at our house yourself. If you send it through the post office they deduct two hundred dollars." If we are to receive gifts from God, most of us would like to have some direct contact, although, of course, some of the gifts of God come to us from the hands and lives of people as imperfect as ourselves.

The giving of spiritual gifts, the *charismata,* is a frequently misunderstood and often controversial teaching of the New Testament. It has the potential for rancor and division within a local congregation and for vibrant life. Sometimes the giving of the gifts is ascribed to the Spirit of God, to God, or to Christ; it doesn't seem to matter. First Corinthians observes, "There are varieties of gifts, but the same Spirit; and there are varieties of service, but the same Lord; and there are varieties of working, but it is the same God who inspires them all in every one" (12:4-6).

A substantial list of these gifts appears in Romans 12:6-8, First Corinthians 12:8-10, First Corinthians 12:28-30, and Ephesians 4:11. This chapter concentrates on verses 7-13 of Ephesians 4 where Christ is said to be the giver of the gifts, of the *charismata*. "Grace was given to each of us according to the measure of Christ's gift." In looking at these several verses I would like to use three headings: grace, gift, goal.

Grace

The frame of reference in this passage is individual men and women within the local congregation. Paul is saying that in its essential nature a congregation is composed of persons who receive the grace of Jesus Christ. Although Paul writes to a particular congregation in the city of Ephesus, by extension and by inspiration he writes to Christians in all times and places.

Grace is one of those big religious ideas we stumble over, like salvation, redemption, or sanctification. It is so big that we can't quite get a handle on it. Can we define it? Sure! "Grace is the free gift of God." Or perhaps this is better: "Grace is the way God freely gives us the divine Self." Someone with a touch of humor said, "Grace is getting something you don't deserve. Mercy is not getting something you do deserve." Walter Wink brings to light the dynamic nature of grace when he writes about being "brought from the death of a world centered in the ego to the life of a world brimming with God."[1]

The theme of grace runs through the New Testament like an interstate highway, from one end to the other, visible everywhere. When Jesus talks about the kingdom of God, for instance, he is talking about the grace-filled presence of God at our own front door, the self-giving presence of God inviting us to step into a new world of awareness. Here are some New Testament passages that help define *grace:*

John 1:14	The Word became flesh and dwelt among us, full of grace and truth.
Romans 6:14	You are not under law but under grace.
Second Corinthians 8:9	You know the grace of our Lord Jesus Christ, that though he was rich, yet for your sake he became poor, so that by his poverty you might become rich.
Ephesians 2:8	By grace have you been saved through faith; and this is not your own doing, it is the gift of God—not because of works, lest any man should boast.

There is a liberating and life-giving feel to these verses. Nevertheless, many of us understand the Christian faith as something demanded from us rather than something given to us. We feel it as obligation rather than opportunity. We experience it as condemnation rather than forgiveness. We see God as the probation officer keeping track of our offenses rather than the counselor trying to win our freedom. Therefore, at some profound level within us, perhaps a subconscious level, we resist a personal surrender to the grace of God. Just as we are often afraid to give ourselves away in love and thus end up missing it, so we are afraid to give ourselves away in faith and end up missing its glorious freedom. How hard it is for us to give up control or to admit personal need. We would rather have a tooth pulled without anesthetic than to admit we are in need. "O God, I need you!" How simple a sentence, but what a struggle in the inner life.

If we have doubts, fears, and questions (and who doesn't?) then we think God cannot handle our hesitation but will write black marks in a book against us. What kind of a God is that? Is that the same God who sent Jesus into the world for me and you? I don't think so. Yes, we can suffer the results of wrong choices, wandering into far countries and squandering our substance on things of no consequence, but God, like the father of the prodigal son, is keeping watch for us from the windows of the kingdom, waiting for us to turn in that direction so that we can be welcomed home. That is the grace of God.

Our text is telling us that grace is the air we breathe in a Christian community. That is why Paul writes, "Grace was given to each of us according to the measure of Christ's gift."

Gift

Out of the ocean of grace, God gives particular gifts to individual men and women. Each person whose life is engaged with God's life in Christ and in creation is gifted—not just the clergy, not just the notable saints of the ages, not just the lay leaders of the congregation who have visibility, but each and every Christian. To use an old but beautiful image, Christ knocks on the heart's door. When we open the door, inviting him to enter, we are graced with his presence. Our own human spirits are kindled by the spirit of Christ. That gracious presence manifests itself in particular gifts we are given. Paul names some of them in our text: "His gifts were that some should be apostles, some prophets, some evangelists, some pastors and teachers." Perhaps it works this way: When Christ takes up residence in the heart, his spirit chooses, focuses, sharpens, and directs some native energy already present within us so that it can be of use in the purposes of God. A transformation happens; an infusion of grace into our human nature.

Let me name some names: Here is Gail, chairwoman of a congregation's membership committee. When a class of prospective members begins to meet, Gail tells something of her own faith story—how she came into engagement with Jesus Christ, the Lord of the church. This turns the new members' class from a formal recitation of names, addresses, and family statistics into a telling of personal stories—why people were coming to the church at this time in their lives, where they were on the journey of faith, what they are hoping for from church involvement. Gail has made it legitimate to talk about personal faith. She is doing the work of an evangelist. It is a gift God has given her.

Here is Dave, a corporate executive. When a daughter was married, he and his wife Pat invited a group of friends to a celebration over dinner. These were the closest people to them in the world. Dave stood up between courses and spoke to and about each person present. He told what the friendship meant and gave the most beautiful, clear, natural, and winsome witness to his faith in Jesus Christ I think I have ever heard anyone give. I don't know what the name of that gift is, but if there is one called "authenticity," Dave has it.

Here is Grace, a widow and elder in her church. A casual observer might describe her as a quintessential grandmother whose native habitat would be the kitchen. But Grace has committed herself to the peace movement. She withholds that part of her taxes which would go to military spending; she works to help Central American refugees; she informs her congregation about legislation affecting national military policy and about action programs for making peace. Not everyone agrees with Grace, but all who know her realize she is speaking out and acting out a prayer for God's shalom for all the world's people. It is a gift God has given her.

Four New Testament listings of the gifts God gives were mentioned above. A comparison of these lists shows both commonality and variety. Prophecy appears in all four lists, teaching in three, several other gifts in two. That's the commonality. Many gifts appear only once. That's the variety. "The variety among the lists shows that there is local variation and considerable freedom for charismatic leadership," according to Wayne A. Meeks.[2] Apparently the list is dynamic and not static, the gifts being given according to the need in a local church situation. A common grace shared by all Christians manifests itself in individual gifts for a particular congregation. Paul writes of "having gifts that differ according to the grace given us" (Rom. 12:6).

It is critically important for the vitality of the local congregation that individual Christians read themselves into these texts. The gifts are available. The Lord of the church is anxious to give them. They do not exist in some unreachable, super-spiritual, almost magical realm. The individual Christian does not have to attain the seventh heaven of spiritual perfection before a gift is given. One way to obtain a gift is to pray for its manifestation and to wait expectantly. The common image is the individual kneeling in prayer and the Spirit descending like a dove to touch and infuse the gift. But that's not the only way. We would do well and learn much if we were to ask ourselves the following questions: Where do I experience Christ's liberating power? Where do the energies of the gospel engage my heart? Where are the growing edges of my spiritual and personal life? What is the church doing that appeals to my inner sensibilities? These questions can lead us to recognize and affirm gifts given by Christ.

Goal

The grace of our Lord Jesus Christ that is to be the pervasive atmosphere of Christian community and the gifts that are given to the members of the community are given for particular reasons. They move toward a central goal. Our text is quite specific: "His gifts were . . . to equip the saints for the work of ministry." Why the gifts? So that the congregation may be equipped to do the work of Christ in the world. This word *equip* is a remarkable word in the original Greek of the text. In medicine it means "to set a broken bone." In politics it means "to bring together opposing factions so that the government can go on." In the New Testament it is used for "mending" fishing nets. The basic idea, then, is to restore something so that it will be able to do what it is supposed to do.

On the one hand, to exercise a spiritual gift is to invest who we are and what God has given us in the local congregation. We are to be a mutually supportive, growth-oriented, faith-strengthening community. We are to help each other, to teach, guide, nourish, correct, inspire, encourage, and love each other for Jesus' sake. Those who are strong in one area may be weak in another and need the gifts of others in the community. Some Christians have an outgoing personal warmth, some feel compassion at deeper levels of life, some have the gift of hospitality, some are keen in mind, some intuitive in spirit. These gifts are to be shared for the strength of the whole body of Christ. Why are these gifts given? For the equipping of the saints and for building up the body of Christ. As each Christian digs deeper foundations in the spiritual life, the whole church grows in power and authenticity. The church, after all, is an organism, the body of Christ.

One could observe that there is a seriousness about receiving and exercising spiritual "energies." But there is an inherent lightness about it as well, an innate enthusiasm that belongs to the very nature of the gospel. Christians love, worship, and serve a risen Christ. We have come through Good Friday to Easter. However dark the powers of death may be, however ominous in our experience at a given time, we know there is a resurrection. Like Abram following the call of God to a new land, we have God's future in our bones. This is not to deny the pain of our mortality but to sketch in the eternal horizon against which we live out our years.

Have you thought about the way the local church gets consumed in institutional maintenance? The list of chores to be done is endless: keeping the books, sweeping the floors, paying the utilities, repairing the buildings, attending the meetings. None of these things is mentioned as a gift in Paul's lists. All the items he sets forth are relational, none are institutional. Yes, we give energy to the visible church with its buildings and programs, but what a sacrifice if we do little else. Why maintain the external forms unless the spirit of God is doing the work of God's new creation in our midst?

We are saying that the reason the gifts are given is for the equipping of Christians for ministry. Our own spiritual and personal growth is an inescapable part of the Christian journey, for without an expanding personal horizon life soon grows dull and repetitious. Having said all of this, still we have not stated the essential goal of the passage. Our personal growing, our building up in the faith, our life of worship and learning all move toward one word in the text: *ministry.* Paul uses the Greek word *diakonia,* best translated as "humble service." There is no gift without task, no calling without commissioning for service. The church, after all, is not a closed circle of like-minded people banded together for moral improvement. It is not basically psychological and social, but missionary and evangelistic. Jesus Christ is not Lord of a cult, but Lord of the world. We are to bear witness to his lordship through *diakonia,* humble and courteous service. This often takes the form of a very concrete and hands-on helping of the poor of the earth. It is with "deeds of love and mercy, [that] The heavenly Kingdom comes."[3] The hospitals the church has built, the multitudes it has taught in its mission schools around the world, the bandages wound by Christian women's groups, the agricultural assistance, the technological help—all this and a hundred other things have been in response to the call to make Christ known, *diakonia!* This is service done at the command of Christ, service modeled after the example of Christ, service enabled through the gifts of Christ.

As Christians, the local congregation is our frame of reference for the life of faith. It is the workshop where we submit ourselves to the Master Craftsman for restoration and renewal. Here we make a mutual commitment to grow together in discipleship. Here we covenant to make the love of Christ tangible and experiential in our world. Here we invest ourselves and live in hope.

Notes

1. Walter Wink, p. 164.
2. Wayne A. Meeks, *The First Urban Christians* (New Haven, CT: Yale University Press, 1984), p. 135.
3. "Lead on, O King Eternal," *The Hymnal,* no. 371.

13. The Head of the Church

4:14-16

Christians are ready to admit that the church is a human community and therefore a flawed community. As in other organizations, there are power struggles, political maneuverings, impure motives, conflicts, and periods of discouragement. Believing that good old First Church down on the corner of Main and Maple could be God's chosen instrument (and you know some of things that have gone on down there) requires a real leap of faith! We admit it: the image the church projects in the world is sometimes less than illustrious.

No definition of the church I have read, however, makes perfection one of the qualifications for a true church. It is Hans Kung's opinion that "any human community, great or small, for whom Jesus Christ is ultimately decisive can be called a Christian Church."[1] And James A. Sanders helps us to look beneath some of the human imperfections, telling us that the true church "is the place of God's presence, from which God calls to us, where reverence is due him, where God reveals his name, where he gives us a mission."[2] Like the burning bush the church is the place where we meet God and begin to see the world with different eyes.

I begin with these general comments on the church because this passage, Ephesians 4:14-16, is such a powerful statement on the essential nature of the church of Jesus Christ. In trying to open up the meaning of the text, I choose three ideas: stance, style, and strength.

Stance

"Speaking the truth in love, we are to grow up in every way into him who is the head, into Christ."

One's stance is the way one stands, the posture one assumes. We could ask about someone's political stance, moral stance, or religious stance. The way a person feels about atomic weapons, taxation, ecology, abortion, racial equality, or sex education in the schools would be the stance that person takes. Our text raises the question, "What is the stance of the Christian?" That is, what is of primary importance? This is not the same as asking, "What is your opinion?" Instead, it is the question, "Who are you really? How do you, as a Christian, respond to the human quandary about life and death, success and failure, faith and doubt, love and hate?"

Let me speak to these questions in the light of the text. First, the Christian stands facing forward into God's future. We are "to grow up in every way into him who is the head, into Christ." Surely that phrase indicates forward movement. There are yesterdays that faith remembers, and they are of critical importance to the Christian story, a story that unfolds as the Jesus story intersects with my own life. I read the Bible; I learn the gospel narrative; I become acquainted with the life, death, and resurrection of Jesus Christ. I am taught and come to grasp the significance of a gospel anchored in human history. Christianity is a faith "built upon the foundation of the apostles and prophets, Christ Jesus himself being the cornerstone" (2:20). I remember yesterday. Yet my stance as a Christian inevitably and irresistibly faces forward into God's tomorrow. A verse in Isaiah states it beautifully,

> Behold, I am doing a new thing;
> now it springs forth, do you not perceive it?
> I will make a way in the wilderness and rivers in the desert.
>
> —43:19

Facing forward into God's future is one way of talking about the hope that lies so close to the core of the Christian faith. The Christian lives in hope because of the belief that this is God's world and especially because of the experience of God present in Jesus Christ. Therefore history is not cyclical, meaningless, and dead-ended. Rather it is the theater where God is directing an immense drama about a world of light called "The Kingdom." God has asked us to be players in the drama and we have accepted. Having accepted, we begin to feel the magnetic powers of that kingdom drawing us onward, powers which we know in our bones belong to life, to light, and to love. They are at work in us, transforming our chaos into order and our night into day. That's when we know what the poet meant when she wrote:

> Earth's crammed with heaven,
> And every common bush afire with God:
> But only he who sees, takes off his shoes.[3]

The Christian stance is forward, facing the coming kingdom. It is a hope by which we are possessed and is, therefore, "a sure and steadfast anchor of the soul" (Heb. 6:19).

In the second place, the Christian stance commits to a lifelong process of growing toward maturity in Jesus Christ. The text says, "We are to grow up in every way into him who is the head." The verse preceding this one cautions against immaturity "so that we may no longer be children, tossed to and fro and carried about with every wind of doctrine." Paul is saying that though there may be shifting winds and crosscurrents in the storms of life, we have an anchoring place, Jesus Christ our rock of certainty. There we find our security, not a smug security that puts all its gears in neutral, but a security that depends on Christ as a truth that can inform and shape all our half-truth and all our falseness. How can I be real? What does it mean to love my neighbor? What do I do with tragedy? What is success? All these questions find rich responses, though not easy responses, in the person of Jesus Christ. As we pursue them through him and through life itself, we "grow up in every way into him who is the head."

The Christian stance turns toward Christ as a compass needle turns toward the magnetic north. Our own internal life, our spirituality, and our psychology need a center of meaning. We lose direction, power, and joy when we lack it. We are, in fact, driven toward committing our lives to something, reposing our faith in something, gathering the scattered energies of our being around something. For the Christian, that commitment has a familiar ring: "Jesus Christ is Lord and Savior." To make that basic confession of faith is to choose him as our "still point of the turning world."[4]

Style

Christians are to speak the truth in love. If all the sermons ever preached on this verse were stacked up, they would probably reach the moon. And if all the parishioners who ever went to sleep listening to these sermons were laid out in a row, they probably would have been a lot more comfortable. But these statistics have no power to deter this writer from yet one more attempt. Did you ever hear a sermon on the love of God that left you feeling clobbered and criticized? Did the preacher wax fierce? Did his neck bulge and his voice crack? Did you ever meet an overzealous witness on the street corner who told you to repent or else? You felt about as much warmth and acceptance as when you got a letter from the IRS wanting to review last year's income tax. Marshall McLuhan was right. "The medium is the message."[5] I take that to mean, at least in part, that the emotional tone being communicated is often stronger than the actual words and therefore becomes the message received. It's a matter of style that concerns Paul when he advises "speaking the truth in love."

We cannot promote belief at the expense of love. We are not to beat people on the head with the gospel nor try to intimidate them into believing. Love requires that we meet people where they are, honor the dignity of each life, earn the right to speak. True, different people need differing styles of approach, but this approach should be always in harmony with the way we see Jesus communicating in the gospels. It is worth remarking that love is the primary gift of the Spirit, Paul's "more excellent way" (1 Cor. 12:31). It is the gift out of which all the other gifts take their shape.

It is also worth remarking that in biblical context love

does not mean sentimental feeling or emotional warmth, but rather concrete action. Love is a verb, for sentiment without action is hollow. Because God loved the world, he *gave* the Son. Because Jesus loved the world he *gave* himself for us. Frederick Buechner says, "Love, not as an excuse for the mushy and innocuous, but love as a summons to battle against all that is unlovely and unloving in the world."[6] Whether they know the reference or not, a lot of people are singing the verse of Isaac Bickerstaffe:

> I care for nobody, not I,
> If no one cares for me.[7]

Christians are not to be among these people. Being loved by God in Christ, we are to pass it along to others. The Christian style is to love concretely for Jesus' sake.

But what about loving those inside the church? What is the style of life together in the Christian congregation? Now we come closer to the chapter title, "The Head of the Church." Let me do my own translation of verse 16: "Christ provides sustenance to the whole church and meets the needs of every member in the way each touches the other." The analogy that runs through this entire passage is that of the church as the body of Christ. This is the focal point of the passage. Christ is head of the whole church, giving it direction and reason for being; Christ is head for every member of the church, providing nourishment and strength so that the whole church grows. We are individuals, but we are a company. There is diversity, but there is unity. There are many gifts, but one Spirit who gives them. This is the church as it was meant to be—a rich diversity of persons owning a common allegiance to Jesus Christ.

The church has something unique to offer to our

culture and to the world. We offer, in Jesus' name, an experience of the presence of God, the good news that our faltering human spirits can be touched and restored by the life-giving spirit of God. That is going to come across as unreal, as some kind of spiritual palaver unless we offer it out of an enraptured heart and out of the midst of an open, honest, and loving fellowship of faith. We must be in our congregational life what we say we are in our creeds; head and heart must be joined together, or forget it, the world will pass us by with a knowing smile.

Part of the way to accomplish this is building a Christian community where each person matters. If we cannot keep straight on this, we will not be able to keep straight on anything. It is a reflection of our love for Christ our head, who loves each with the patient and suffering love of God.

Our style, then, in the congregation, is open and accepting. As we build trust, admitting our common weakness, we discover an honesty aimed at mutual growth toward mature discipleship. We do not do this merely for our own sake, but for the sake of the world. We are not a mutual admiration society, nor do we practice closed circuit spirituality. Chosen and gifted by the Spirit, we grow in faith so that, strengthened in love, we may be able to live and speak the gospel in the world God loves.

Strength

"Christ provides sustenance to the whole church and meets the needs of every member in the way each touches the other."

It seems that an astronomer and a minister fell into discussion about religion. The astronomer said, "Would you like to know what I believe about religion?" "Yes," said the minister, "I would be very interested." The astronomer replied, "It all boils down to this, do unto others as you would have them do unto you." "My," said the minister, "Isn't that something! Would you like to know what I believe about astronomy?" "Well, yes," said the astronomer. "It all boils down to this," he said, "Twinkle, twinkle little star, how I wonder what you are!"

Whether in matters of science or faith, light-headed answers are insufficient. Our text issues a call to maturity, a call which is inherent and unavoidable for anyone who wishes to pursue a journey of faith. Our perception of who Christ is and our commitment to him and to the church is to deepen with the years. Substance and vitality must be hallmarks in Christian witness. Paul is telling us that there is an energy in the church leading us toward maturity, a strength upon which we can draw. Here is what is being said: First of all, Jesus Christ, as head of the body, is the source of our strength. Paul has a high Christology, as *The Expositor's Greek New Testament* points out:

> The idea then (of the text) would be that it is only by being *in relation* to Christ that we can grow. . . . This means more than that we are to grow into *resemblance* to Him, or that our growth is to be according to His *example.* It means that as He is the source *from* which the grace or power comes that makes it possible for us to grow, He is also the *object* and *goal* to which our growth in its every stage must look and is to be directed.[8]

In speaking of the essential energy coursing through the body of the church Paul uses a word, *energeia,* describing the way God acts in Christ. It is a strength divinely infused into the church's life, a grace to be received so that the transforming presence of Christ may mark the church's journey across time. Secondly, it is not only as each member of the body receives strength from the head that the church grows toward maturity, but also as that strength is passed from life to life within the congregation. As we touch each other in the church, as our lives come into contact through worship, mission, and fellowship, as we share doubt and affirmation, joy and sorrow, we are strengthened by other Christians. We feel the body-life. We remember Jesus' promise, "Where two or three are gathered in my name, there am I in the midst of them" (Matt. 18:20). This is why the church can aptly be described as "the beloved community."

One cannot miss the striking intimacy in this Ephesian passage nor resist an exhortation: As long as the church is a polite religious society gathered together for tasteful liturgy and moral encouragement, as long as the members build a fellowship no deeper than light social contact, as long as the cement of church life is social and economic homogeneity rather than an essential allegiance to Jesus Christ as Lord, the strength and vitality of the church will remain a mystery and its mission will be short-circuited. It remains the mandate of every local congregation to keep on asking how Christ is the head of the church.

Notes

1. Hans Kung, *On Being a Christian* (New York: Doubleday & Company, 1976), p. 125.

2. James A. Sanders, *God Has a Story Too* (Philadelphia: Fortress Press, 1979), p. 57.

3. Elizabeth Barrett Browning, *Aurora Leigh*, bk. 7.

4. T. S. Eliot, "Burnt Norton," in *The Complete Poems and Plays, 1909-1950*, p. 121.

5. Marshall McLuhan, *Understanding Media: The Extensions of Man* (New York: McGraw-Hill Book Company, 1964), p. vii.

6. Frederick Buechner, *The Hungering Dark* (Minneapolis: Seabury Press, 1969), p. 42.

7. Isaac Bickerstaffe, "There Was a Jolly Miller Once," in *The Oxford Book of Eighteenth Century Verse* (Oxford: Oxford University Press, 1926, reprinted 1971), p. 417.

8. W. Robertson Nicoll, ed., *The Expositor's Greek New Testament*, vol. 3 (Grand Rapids, MI: Wm. B. Eerdmans Publishing Company, 1952), pp. 335-6.

14. The Author of the New Nature

4:17-32

Across a broad range of literature one can find a cry for the old to pass away and the new to come. Tennyson's "Maud" contains these lines:

> Ah God, for a man with heart, head, hand,
> Like some of the simple great ones gone
> For ever and ever by,
> One still strong man in a blatant land,
> Whatever they call him, what care I,
> Aristocrat, democrat, autocrat—one
> Who can rule and dare not lie.
>
> And ah for a man to arise in me,
> That the man I am may cease to be.[1]

In Peter Shaffer's play, *Equus*, are the lines: "All reined up in old language and old assumptions, straining to jump cleanhoofed onto a whole new track of being I only suspect is there. I can't see it, because my educated, average head is being held at the wrong angle."[2] In Fritjof Capra's *The Turning Point* we read: "As in every self-organizing system, the restoration of balance and flexibility may often be achieved through self-transcendence—breaking through a state of instability or crisis to new forms of organization."[3]

Tennyson is a classic English poet, Shaffer a contemporary playright, Capra a physicist, and each in his own kind of language talks about the old passing away and the new taking its place. This is a theme not uncommon to the scriptures. Ezekiel prophesies: "I will give them one heart, and put a new spirit within them; I will take the stony heart out of their flesh and give them a heart of flesh . . . and they shall be my people, and I will be their God" (11:19-20). Ephesians says this: "Put off your old nature which belongs to your former manner of life and is corrupt . . . and be renewed in the spirit of your minds, and put on the new nature, created after the likeness of God."

There is, is there not, a fascination with such a possibility, that we might exchange the old for the new; or better yet, that we might escape from the old into the new? Is there some secret door we might enter, some mystery that can be revealed to us that will move us into a new dimension of reality? Paul seems to think so and attempts to show us the way in the fourth chapter of Ephesians. He speaks about the old nature, lists its characteristics, and issues a command: "Put off the old nature!" Then he issues a second command: "Put on the new nature!" He then describes what it is. Let's try to follow him through this second half of Ephesians 4.

The Characteristics of the Old Nature

Paul is pretty good at setting up contrasts between the life of the pagan Roman world he lives in and the life he has found in Christ. For him it is no less than the difference between darkness and light or death and life.

Here is a graphic translation to heighten the contrast. Paul describes the old nature, fallen nature, darkened nature, like this:

> No longer conduct yourselves as do the Gentiles in the futility of their mind. Intellectually they are blacked out. Because of their inherent refusal to know [God] and of the petrifaction of their hearts, they are excluded from the life of God. In their insensitive state they have given themselves over to debauchery in order to do all filthy things and still ask for more.[4]

Paul is warning the Ephesian believers away from a lifestyle that permeates the pagan world of the day—a lifestyle that has broad cultural approval and acceptance because it is condoned and promoted by the Roman Empire itself. Roman state religion is declining in energy while fertility religions are gaining strength. The drama and mystery of these religions, wedded as they are to human sexuality, are powerful beyond our imagination. Paul knows that the celebration of physical sensation at the very heart of a religion is ultimately destructive, incapable of leading anyone to the grace and love of God.

If you know anything about the Old Testament and the desperate struggle of Israel to keep its worship of God free from the practices of the surrounding fertility religions, then you can appreciate the feelings of Paul as he wanders past the Greek and Roman temples of his day. He finds the practices utterly abhorrent to the point of disbelief. How can this be happening? How can a human being be so degraded, with knowledge of God so darkened that this is considered worship? And Paul lets us know how he feels as he describes the pagan lifestyle. Let me pick out some of his phrases.

Futility: "No longer conduct yourselves as do the Gentiles in the futility of their mind." It's a strong word in the Greek original implying emptiness, foolishness, and lack of purpose.[5] Our word *vacuous* might be equivalent. Emptiness implies lack of meaning, lack of commitment to worthy goals that engage the heart and mind. It goes hand in hand with that awful word *boredom*. This is it in a nutshell: The pagan worship and lifestyle of Paul's day is characterized by emptiness and boredom. It is shallow and profoundly unsatisfying. After all, the attempt to wring meaning from life solely in terms of satisfying physical desires ends in triviality. You don't have to have a lot of life experience to realize that! Rollo May puts this into words that apply to our own time when he identifies "what *is* tragic in our day, namely the complete confusion, banality, ambiguity, and vacuum of ethical standards and the consequent inability to act."[6]

Blindness: "Intellectually they are blacked out." The literal translation is "darkened in their understanding," a condition opposite to the one Paul attributes to followers of Jesus Christ, "having the eyes of your hearts enlightened" (Eph. 1:18). Paul is saying that there is a land of darkness in which people dwell, a shadow land that hides the mercy and love of God. They have given themselves to principles and practices that obscure the face of God and to powers that hold them in bondage. In the words of the text, they are under the dominion of the "old nature."

Now hang in there, because this gets worse before it gets better. There is a third characterization Paul gives of pagan life and worship.

Hardness of heart: In the words of Markus Barth's translation, Paul speaks of "the petrifaction of their hearts." The Greek word Paul uses originally meant "harder than marble" and then came to mean "without feeling or sensitivity." In the Bible, the heart refers to human nature and character. It is the spring from which our actions flow. It is to the heart that God speaks, and the heart that decides for or against God. God gave Saul a new heart when he chose him as king over Israel (1 Sam. 10:9). God promises to give Israel a new heart in the eleventh chapter of Ezekiel: "I will take the stony heart out of their flesh and give them a heart of flesh" (v. 19). Paul is saying that pagan life and worship petrifies the heart so that no word from God can be heard or obeyed. It is for this reason that Paul declares, "They are alienated from the life of God."

Paul ends his thought with a flourish: "In their insensitive state they have given themselves over to debauchery in order to do all filthy things and still ask for more." That's quite a sentence! Paul is talking about outrageous behavior without limit or restraint, a surrender to sensation that is never satisfied and keeps on descending to lower and lower levels. If you know anything of the Rome of the emperor Caligula, you will get the idea.

Is this kind of scripture uncomfortable? Is Paul stretching it? Not on your life! He is talking about an attitude always ready to sacrifice one's neighbor to one's own desires. The sale of illegal drugs is a contemporary example. This is so widespread in our culture that writers or preachers know they are addressing some people who have had or are having experience with drugs. Those who are experiencing drugs participate in a system that is always ready to sacrifice neighbor for profit. Those who sell the drugs are not concerned over the addiction or possible death of those who buy. They simply don't care. Talk about the erosion of character; talk about moral insensitivity; talk about self-interest! What were Paul's words? Futility, intellectual blackout, heart of stone—Hey! Not so far off!

Want a better contemporary example yet? Author Michael Satchell writes an article called, "Kids for Sale." He writes, "Across America, there are tens of thousands of children—boys and girls—working as prostitutes. . . . Kids are for sale everywhere, part of the continuing national tragedy of America's runaway and throwaway child population."[7] Using data provided by 595 police departments in fifty states, the author estimates there are between one hundred thousand and two hundred thousand adolescent prostitutes, with a median age of fifteen. These are children who have run away, are abandoned, or who have been forced out of their homes. Over half of them who have been on the streets for more than a month become involved in granting sexual favors for pay. One of the youngsters, seventeen, had been a hustler on Santa Monica Boulevard in Los Angeles for five years. He said, "The average person can't imagine what goes on."

What did you say, Paul? "In their insensitive state they have given themselves over to debauchery in order to do all filthy things and still ask for more." People taking advantage of these children are ready to sacrifice them to their own desires.

Paul's words are not limited to various sorts of sexual indulgence. Impurity is broader than that, applying to lack of restraint in satisfying personal desires. In our culture it would apply to all the stock swindles we read about, government or business leaders with their hand in the till, and the amazingly versatile ways in which people rip off their neighbors. The god they worship is their own self-gratification. All of these things fall under what Paul calls the "old nature." Having listed them, he issues a dramatic imperative: "Strip off your old nature!" Translations that say "take off" or "put off" don't do justice to the energy of Paul's language. Having described the excesses of those who stop at nothing to satisfy their desires, Paul is dramatic: "Strip off your old nature"—like a suit of clothes! Get rid of it and don't waste any time!

There is an infinite weariness in the paganism of the Roman Empire. It is morally bankrupt, shallow, trivial, and knows little of the deeper reaches of the human spirit. That is becoming true in some segments of our world. We need to hear it now as they heard it then: "Strip off your old nature!" In Gail Sheehy's best seller, *Passages,* a man named Aaron was a fashion designer close to the top of his field. But with all his affluent success, he wasn't happy. He was having marital trouble, physical trouble, and emotional trouble, and he was close to internal collapse. In therapy he examines his life, and in a reflective moment confesses, "What I really want is a clear, unencumbered beginning."[8] That's an appeal for conversion if ever there was one. Here is a man who wants to exchange the old for the new. His life situation has brought him to a place where the words of Paul have a dynamic relevance. "Strip off the old nature!"

The first command of Paul means nothing without the second, nor will the second stand alone. Christianity cannot be defined on the basis of abstentions, but on affirmations. In Garrison Keillor's *Lake Wobegon Days,* Catholic children have been fretting about what they will have to give up for Lent and are apparently waiting for nuns to give the word. A twelve-year-old muses, "Ha! Easy for nuns to talk about giving up things. That's what nuns do for a living."[9]

The real business of this passage, its glowing center, is

the second imperative: "Put on the new nature!" Or, "Clothe yourselves in the nature of Christ." Are you tired of the old? Do you feel used up by the old? Do you feel trapped in the old? Have you had enough of always seeking more and never being satisfied? "Put on the new nature!" Don't delay. Do it today. A lot of people to whom Paul speaks, and God through him, are at the end of their rope. They need to hear the command of the text so that they will surrender their lives to Christ.

Maybe "the new nature" isn't the best translation. It really says, "The new Man." And it is surely true that *Man* should be capitalized, for Jesus is the new Man, understood as the new Adam, head of the new creation. Jesus is the Man for the new age, the new hope, and the new life. The appeal is for us to clothe ourselves in the nature of God's new Man. Formerly we lived for self-gratification or self-advantage, but now a new reality has come.

The Characteristics of the New Nature

Paul lists three characteristics dealing with truth, anger, and foul talk.

Speaking the Truth: Paul looks at the surrounding culture and sees it riddled with falsehood. People are altering the truth, manipulating the truth, and distorting it for their own advantage. You have to pass what they are saying through a strainer to decide what is real and what is not. Falsehood puts distance between people and creates suspicion and negativity. It breaks down human community. Lewis Thomas says that telling a lie sets off a kind of smoke alarm in the brain that can be recorded on a lie detector. He concludes that falsehood is stressful and in a physiological sense unnatural.[10] I cannot imagine a worse condemnation than for someone to say about me, "He is false." These words of Paul about speaking the truth are addressed in particular to members of the Ephesian church. He wants honesty to be a hallmark of the Christian community, a distinguishing characteristic of those who follow Jesus, who is "the way, and the truth, and the life" (John 14:6).

Anger Does Not Prevail: Plainly, anger can be a deadly and disruptive force. It can destroy the fellowship of Christ's church, sapping energy and direction from the Christian mission in the world. Ecclesiastes says, "Be not quick to anger, for anger lodges in the bosom of fools" (7:9). Paul tells the Colossians, "put them all away: anger, wrath, malice, slander" (3:8), listing anger first. He understands there will be disagreements, for he struggles with it in his churches, but he counsels that there be tenderness and forgiveness in the midst of it all.

No More Foul Talk: This is difficult for many people. It sounds so moralistic. We recall lectures against bad words or getting a dirty mouth washed out with soap. Can't we tell any more spicy stories? The idea behind "foul talk" is the idea of rottenness, as in a piece of rotten fruit. Since it is rotten, it is worthless and useless, leading to no good end. I don't know about you, but I hear a lot of worthless talking. Some of it offends me worse than the so-called bad words. This is the complaining talk, the grousing, the moaning and groaning, the "ain't it awful" talk that tears things down and sows the seeds of discontent. It offers no solutions, takes no positive action, but simply wrings its hands. "Calamity howling" is a particularly descriptive phrase. "Put that aside," Paul says. "Be kind to one another, tender-hearted, forgiving one another as God in Christ forgave you." This is a lifestyle that nurtures, that builds people up, that affirms and strengthens, accentuating the positive. Hey! Go for it! Take the risk of affirmation. In another letter, Paul says about Jesus, "All the promises of God find their Yes in him" (2 Cor. 1:20).

To summarize: The appeal of these last sixteen verses of Ephesians 4 is to clothe ourselves in the new nature. The author of the new nature is Jesus Christ. We are to strip off the old, the used up, the worthless, the chains with which we are bound; and we are to put on the new nature, which is dressed in all the colors of the rainbow.

Notes

1. Alfred Lord Tennyson, *Maud*, canto 10, stanza 5-6.
2. Peter Shaffer, *Equus* (New York: Avon Books, Bard Books, 1974), p. 22.
3. Fritjof Capra, *The Turning Point* (New York: Simon & Schuster, 1982), p. 396.
4. Markus Barth, *Ephesians 4-6*, p. 498.
5. Ibid. p. 499.
6. Rollo May, *Love and Will* (New York: W.W. Norton & Company, 1969), p. 110.
7. Michael Satchell, "Kids for Sale," *Parade Magazine*, 20 July 1986, p. 4.
8. Gail Sheehy, *Passages* (New York: E.P. Dutton, 1974), p. 340.
9. Garrison Keillor, *Lake Wobegon Days* (New York: Viking Press, Inc., 1985), p. 226.
10. Lewis Thomas, *Late Night Thoughts on Listening to Mahler's Ninth Symphony* (New York: Viking Press, Inc., 1983), p. 128.

V

SENT FOR THE INDIVIDUAL BELIEVER

15. In the Culture

5:1-20

Paul turns to moral and ethical questions in this fifth chapter of Ephesians, to conduct, and to Christian lifestyle in the midst of a degenerate pagan culture. In verses 3-14, he addresses the immersion of Ephesian life in destructive sexuality. If the modern reader winces at language that seems laced with negatives, then that reader is unaware of the nature of sexual practice in Ephesus and elsewhere in the empire. Let me try to lift the curtain on the moral decay that held much of the Roman Empire in its grasp. My outline of Sholem Asch's description of Antioch holds true for Ephesus and other urban centers: The river Orontes flowed into the city of Antioch and its winding banks were a joy to see. Cypress, laurel and oleander trees lined the water's edge, and on either side green meadows lay in sunlight, set with bright beds of jasmine, lilies, violets and crimson poppies. But this blossoming paradise had been turned into something else. Among the trees and in the meadows were many gardens dedicated to a wide assortment of gods and goddesses. Some of the gardens came right down to the water's edge, where eunuch priests clashed their cymbals at passing boats, beckoning travelers to stop for worship in the hidden groves. A temple to the sun god, Apollo, was the most notable shrine, built on the river bank five miles from the city. This was the central gathering place of the consecrated priests and priestesses who sold their bodies on the steps of the temple. They lay around the sacred altars waiting for pilgrims to come and do reverence to the idol. The small fee for their sacred prostitution was collected by temple officials and supported the worship and the worship place.

Any Jews traveling on the boats covered their eyes so they would not see what was happening in the groves and closed their ears so the sound of the cymbals, the fever of the drums, and the noise of the people might not be heard. The smell of the incense, the heavy scent of perfume and aromatic oils were, however, more difficult to escape. Every Jew spat three times and recited the saying: "Let the abomination be laid waste."

Off the ships, on the land, up close were scenes that would make New York's infamous Broadway & 42nd Street look mild. Boat after boat spilled out its cargo of pilgrims come to worship in the embrace of these servants of the divinities. The temple prostitutes held out their arms to passersby, smiled their crimson smiles out of their vacant faces, and hid their diseases behind cosmetics, offering to satisfy any whim or desire. Men dressed as women, women dressed as men, every form of perversion—it was a scene of frantic lust, heavy and oppressive. There was a desperateness about it, this seeking for satisfaction of the body that ended only in deadness of the spirit. It was empty, decadent, with no redeeming grace, like an Old Testament Sodom.[1]

In the midst of this moral deadness, the life of Christ began to blossom like a fresh springtime; in the midst of this darkness the light of Christ began to shine. The contrast was dramatic! Perhaps that is the first thing that jumps out of the text.

The Contrast

The Bible is full of talk about these two opposites, darkness and light. We first hear about it in the creation account in Genesis. James Weldon Johnson gives a poetic interpretation:

> And God stepped out on space,
> And he looked around and said:
> I'm lonely—
> I'll make me a world.
>
> And far as the eye of God could see
> Darkness covered everything,
> Blacker than a hundred midnights
> Down in a cypress swamp.
>
> Then God smiled,
> And the light broke,
> And the darkness rolled up on one side,
> And the light stood shining on the other,
> And God said: That's good![2]

For the most part, however, darkness and light are interpreted figuratively and not literally, not simply light and dark as day and night, but as spiritual darkness and illumination. You hear it in verses like John 3:19: "This is the judgment, that the light has come into the world, and men loved darkness rather than light, because their deeds were evil." You also hear it in Isaiah: "They will look to the earth, but behold, distress and darkness, the gloom of anguish; and they will be thrust into thick darkness" (8:22). This is written during a time of political chaos. Assyria has overrun northern Israel, and in desperation the people turn from God to consult wizards and mediums who say they can consult with the dead. National and spiritual turmoil reigns. But a spiritual revelation floods the prophet's mind so that he is able to see beyond the present trouble:

> The people who walked in darkness
> have seen a great light;
> those who dwelt in a land of deep darkness,
> on them has light shined.
>
> —9:2

How are we twentieth-century Christians to read this first century contrast of pagan and Christian sexual lifestyles in Ephesians 5? What is there in this passage that is as true for us as it was for the Ephesian church? Paul uses a lead-in statement: "Walk in love, as Christ loved us and gave himself up for us." Let me interpret: "Live according to the vision and experience of Christ. Don't let the culture steal this vision from you. Don't let the culture jam you into its mold. Don't absorb the cultural values into your bones by osmosis. Follow Jesus. Establish your Christian identity and lifestyle. The way of Christ is not sexual license but self-giving love." Notice the tone with which Paul speaks. He doesn't sound like a dean of students laying down rules for the dormitory. He doesn't sound like a parent making house rules for a precocious teenager. This is not a scolding passage or a shaming passage but a passage that joyfully and triumphantly proclaims a total vision of life under the lordship of Jesus Christ. It is set in contrast to life under the prevailing morality of the Roman Empire. The Christian does not invest the whole person in the appetites of the body. That is too narrow, too incomplete, and too impoverished a way to live. When Paul counsels against fornication, when he says, in effect, "Don't squander your time majoring on the minors of coarse talk and behavior," he is contrasting the moral poverty of Ephesian life with "the unsearchable riches of Christ" (Eph. 3:8).

What about sexuality today? Where does this Ephesian text find its contemporary applications? Recall that we went through a sexual revolution in the sixties and seventies. It was a part of the rebellion against major institutions: government, school, family, church. All were under attack for rigidity and unresponsiveness to human need and human feeling. One should admit there were significant pieces of truth in the rebellion. Institutions do not exist for their own sake, but for the sake of the persons they serve and with whom they are involved. The mood of the time was to throw off the old restrictions for a new and exciting freedom. Yes, certain Victorian attitudes had suppressed sexuality in an unhealthy way so that it was difficult to accept the physical body and its appetites as part of God's creation. I heard somebody say that it was God who invented sexuality in the first place.

However, as in most rebellions, things tend to go too far in the other direction, and a lot of things were giving the swing added momentum: modern means of contraception, effective treatment for the social diseases, liberalized divorce laws, legalized abortion, and a more healthy acceptance of our human sexuality. As a result, our culture has removed most of the obstacles to a public display of sexuality—movies, magazines, bedroom novels, television, advertising, adult book stores, go-go bars—it permeates the culture. One author talked about "the repeal of reticence."[3] Strange, isn't it, that while the culture still upholds the sanctity of the marriage bond and fidelity within marriage, that same culture gives every enticement to forsake those commitments. While most parents are trying to teach their teenagers a sane approach to sexuality, nearly everything in the teenager's world encourages sexual activity.

What we are experiencing in our culture, then, is a trivialization of sexuality. Making it a marketplace commodity extracts both its meaning and mystery. We do this when we separate sexuality from the rest of life, treating it as a thing in itself, not seeing it in the context of enduring commitment and responsibility. Maybe all those manuals, the Masters and Johnson magnifying glass on sexual practice and the Kinsey reports, are one indication of trivialization, the trend toward analysis and factuality. Hidden in there someplace is the false promise that if I just possess enough information, I have the answer. But that's not so. Knowledge helps, but it is the interpersonal, the mutual self-giving, the capacity for depth relationship, and therefore the personal maturity that are critical. Sexuality is organic, a part of the whole, one section of our human nature. It belongs within the context of our humanness. Sexuality is created by God and seeps through the whole of human life lived under God.

What happened in Ephesian culture is happening also in today's culture: a spiritual vacuum and emptiness of life. Pursuit of material and physical satisfaction at the expense of spiritual and psychic meaning inevitably leads to emptiness. To say this plainly, when we leave God out, we lose touch with who we are.

F. Scott Fitzgerald, in *The Great Gatsby,* gives us a glimpse of emptiness in one of his characters:

> "You see I think everything's terrible anyhow," she went on in a convinced way. "Everybody thinks so—the most advanced people. And I *know.* I've been everywhere and seen everything and done everything." Her eyes flashed around her in a defiant way . . . and she laughed with thrilling scorn. "Sophisticated—God, I'm sophisticated!"[4]

So where does all this leave the Christian in this sex-saturated secular culture? The direction pointed out by Paul remains valid. He speaks directly about his culture, mentioning many of the things we might expect when the subject comes up: coarseness, current sexual practice outside marriage, vulgarity. In the face of the Ephesian sexual circus this is his advice: "Let there be thanksgiving." What a strange thing to say! Why thanksgiving as a response? Because it is a corrective to the obsession of the culture. Thanks for the gift of life, for the wonder of ourselves, body and soul, for God's world around us. How incredible it all is. And above all, thanks for the gift of Jesus Christ, himself flesh and blood, God's great affirmation of our humanity. Thanks is the posture of the whole person, the Christian receiving all as from the hand of God.

Conduct

Marcus Barth translates verse 8 to read, "Conduct yourselves as children of light." That's what "walk as children of light" means. I react negatively to the word *conduct,* and perhaps I have some company among you. It carries with it the overtone of parental admonition. "Now remember, Filbert, conduct yourself like a little gentleman!" I'm sure that made Filbert want to go out behind the house to make faces. Or, "Philomena, your conduct better be appropriate when the pastor comes to call." I'm sure that made Philomena want to kick him in the shins. If you feel your palms beginning to sweat when I talk about conduct, just put your feet flat on the floor and draw a deep breath. The conduct we are talking about is a Christian lifestyle spontaneously generated by the love of Christ within, not by the demands of external authority. Once the light of Christ begins to shine within, life begins to change. This is not a matter of hearing lectures about right living, but a matter of personal transformation into the image and likeness of Christ. Paul does not strike the note of moral reproof, but the note of the inherent power of the gospel to change life from the inside out. Our text rejoices in that power in statements like "Awake, O sleeper, and arise from the dead, and Christ shall give you light." Second Corinthians voices the same native energy: "Now the Lord is the Spirit, and where the Spirit of the Lord is, there is freedom. And we all, with unveiled face, beholding the glory of the Lord, are being changed into his likeness from one degree of glory to another; for this comes from the Lord who is the Spirit" (3:17–19).

Let me say it again: Christian conduct is not a religious code imposed from without, all full of rules and regulations, but a change in the inner life brought by the presence of the spirit of Christ. Yes, there is room for instruction in right living, but it is Christ, the divine alchemist, who changes our base metal into gold. His freedom breaks our chains. His peace brings rest to our restlessness. His presence brings meaning to our years. His forgiving love enables us to forgive and to love in his name.

Perhaps an analogy will help. Here is a wholesale

diamond company that sells its jewels around the world. There are people who sort, analyze, x-ray, cut, and polish the diamonds. But only one person grades the diamonds, putting them in the proper trays. Some are poor, fair, good, or excellent. How does the one who grades the stones maintain good judgment in handling so many? Don't they all look alike after awhile? That person wears a perfect diamond, studying it through an eyepiece every twenty minutes. It is the perfect diamond that reveals the flaws in the many stones analyzed and graded. The application is simple: For Christians, Christ is the perfect pattern for our humanity—his strength and gentleness, his clarity and compassion, his grace and freedom, his centering in the love of God. By him we measure our lives, discovering not only a pattern to emulate, but a presence to excite our wonder and love. This is the way we move from darkness to light.

When I see people spending their whole life energy on the acquisition of material things, when I see them chasing the elusive pleasures of the body apart from spiritual and relational substance, when I watch drug and alcohol abuse worsen, when I see the whole world trembling under the threat of nuclear annihilation, when I admit how much darkness in me is still unclaimed by the light, then I hear in fresh ways the biblical call, "Walk as children of light."

There are those who are called by God to live in the relative seclusion of a spiritual community, a place apart from the mainstream of life, but most of us who take the name Christian will have to work out our calling in the midst of a secular culture where contemporary values often contradict Christian values. We will need to establish our identity as Christians by being part of a Christian community that worships in the midst of that culture, that bears confident witness to the life in Christ, and that joyfully obeys God's call to serve the life of the world for Jesus' sake.

Notes

1. Sholem Asch, *The Apostle* (New York: G.P. Putnam's Sons, 1943), pp. 298-9.
2. James Weldon Johnson, "The Creation," in *God's Trombones* (New York: The Viking Press, Inc., 1927), p. 17.
3. Christopher Lasch, *The Culture of Narcissism* (New York: W.W. Norton & Company, 1979), p. 191.
4. F. Scott Fitzgerald, *The Great Gatsby* (New York: Charles Scribner's Sons, 1925), p. 18.

16. In the Home

5:21-6:9

Having just looked at Christian identity and lifestyle in Ephesian culture, especially with regard to current sexual practice, Paul now opens a door on the privacy of the Christian home. What are the implications of the life in Christ for marriage, he asks, for raising children, and for relationship between slaves and masters? How does Jesus, whom Paul preaches as Lord of all, shape life under the roof of one's own home in the most intimate of human relationships? It is inevitable that these questions be asked against the background of current norms, just as the question of sexuality was raised in relation to those norms. Whatever our generation, first century or twentieth, we are profoundly influenced by the surrounding culture.

While this chapter gives particular attention to Christian marriage, Paul's introductory statement in verse 21, "Be subject to one another out of reverence for Christ," covers 5:22-6:9 and includes parent-child and master-slave relationships as well. It is not in any offhanded manner that Paul begins as he does. His sentence is meant to govern the material to follow and is of primary importance in interpreting what follows, deserving careful comment.

Paul's theology of relationships is plain enough: Christians are to be subject to one another for one reason—*reverence* for Christ. If we are to come to grips with this passage, we must look carefully at this word, *reverence*. The King James Version translates it as "fear." What does Paul mean? Why didn't he talk about the love of Christ instead of the fear of Christ? Maybe the Old Testament will help us. Psalm 111:10 says, "The fear of the Lord is the beginning of wisdom." Exodus 20 portrays Moses bringing down the twin tables of the law from the smoking summit of Sinai and saying to the people, "Do not fear; for God has come to prove you, and that the fear of him may be before your eyes, that you may not sin" (v. 20). Isaiah's soaring vision of God "high and lifted up" (6:1) makes him cry out in fear, "Woe is me! For I am lost; for I am a man of unclean lips, . . . for my eyes have seen the King, the Lord of hosts!" (6:5). While this transcendent language seems native more to the Old Testament, the New is by no means without it. Luke describes the reaction of the crowds after Jesus had healed a paralytic. "Amazement seized them all, and they glorified God and were filled with awe, saying, 'We have seen strange things today'" (5:26). "Awe" is a translation of the common Greek word for fear.

Can we feel what all these writers mean? Does their experience of God's majesty and transcendence correspond to our own? Perhaps a contemporary parallel will help. Toward the end of the movie *Close Encounters of the Third Kind,* the hero and heroine, drawn irresistibly by inner forces, lie hidden on a mountain. They wait for they know not what—other beings from other worlds. A landing field has been prepared by the United States government and ringed with heavy security. It is night. They wait. Then streaks of light flash by, satellite spacecraft, and finally, bigger than five football fields, a mothership descends, a ship of such proportion, such grandeur, and such wonder that every observer stands rooted to the ground. Utterly terrified and utterly fascinated, they watch. The huge ship hovers and sends its message in musical code; the field replies, and the ship lands. A great door swings down, emitting a light so brilliant that none can look without dark glasses. Beings of light descend, otherworldly, beneficent. So profound is the experience for all the humans, so overpowering in its immensity, that no word is spoken throughout the visit.

The impact of this encounter is an analogy in kind to what the Bible means when it says, "The fear of the Lord is the beginning of wisdom." This is not a fear that runs away but a fear that is irresistibly drawn toward the mystery and majesty of what it beholds. It is a mystery that lights up the biblical page: There is a kingdom, there is a world of light, there is a creative power, there is an enveloping presence permeating everything, an all-knowing and all-loving Being whom no word can describe or contain, whom we call God. From time to time our darkness dissipates so that God's glory is glimpsed at some burning bush or other, so that we know the world is more than what we can see with our eyes or touch with our hands. Once that meeting occurs for you, in however dramatic or quiet a way, you are never the same again. It is as if a seed of everlasting light were planted within you, a seed that must grow and permeate your very self. Then, having yourself been met by God, no meeting you have with anyone else will be unaffected. Once forgiven, accepted, welcomed, loved, understood, lifted up, made new, and given hope, it will be less likely that you will be cruel, uncaring, unforgiving, or grasping in your relationships with others.

That lights up the text for me. "Be subject to one another out of reverence for Christ." My relationship with Jesus Christ, Son of the Most High, whom I call Lord and Savior, affects my relationship with everyone else. Paul doesn't let us off easy here. He's not talking about the newsboy who delivers the *Ephesus Daily Times* or the clerk at the Rent-a-Camel service in Jerusalem; if so, he means them only secondarily. Husbands and wives, parents and children, slaves and masters—how do we treat those closest to us? Notice that the intent of Paul's writing is pastoral. He is not writing abstract religious principle here but giving help for daily life in the home. "Try to model your closest personal relationships on Christ" is what he is saying.

Now let's look at this more difficult phrase, "Be subject to one another." "Well," you say, "that'll be the day!" We don't want to be subject to anybody because most of us would rather play first fiddle than second fiddle. Being first isn't everything, but it sure beats being second! Be subject to my husband? Ha! Teenagers subject to parents? Ha! Husbands subject to wives? Double ha! Let's keep straight on Paul's opening statement, which governs the rest of the text. We are talking here about mutual subjection.

Let me try to keep from being dull in explaining the imperative "Be subject." It's not the best translation, since the Greek word does not imply subservience or inferiority. It does not mean to eat humble pie, to bow and scrape, or to serve as someone's doormat. The primary meaning is "to arrange in order." The word was used of a military line of battle. Because you were in front rank did not mean you were the most important. The archers, for instance, were not more important than the spearmen. Each was arranged for the good of all, each for the success of their mutual endeavor. Here's another thing to keep in mind when interpreting "Be subject." Wayne Meeks points out that in the Roman society of the day, "the hierarchically ordered household . . . was regarded as fundamental."[1] He is talking about a rigid system of authority in the home: "those who rule (males, parents, owners) and those who are subordinate (women, children, slaves)."[2] Paul does not want the church to be accused of what Roman writers were accusing novel religious cults of the day, "that they corrupt households and hence threaten the basis of the whole social fabric."[3] Paul was as convinced as the secular writers of his time that a stable household with enduring commitments of the family members to each other was of primary importance. No one who reads the Old Testament could fail to affirm this as the will of God. Like everything else in life, however, Paul cannot look at the nature of family living without seeing it transfused with the light and love of Christ. That's why he begins as he does: "Be subject to one another out of reverence for Christ." This is an intriguing imperative. Surely Paul is comparing and contrasting family relationships in the culture with family relations in the Christian home. He gets clobbered in our day for being conservative, but this text is anything but conservative. It is, in fact, radical. What was the order of life in his day? Patriarchal, and therefore static. There were rigid laws, fixed social patterns that made the man king of the hill and master of his own home with absolute power, even the power of death over his children. The woman had few legal rights; she could not divorce her husband but could be divorced by him. Can you imagine how this sounded in that world, "Be subject to one another"?

In place of fixed law, of a hierarchical model of family relationships, Paul fashions a relational model of startling intimacy, a model built on God's purposes in creation and in Christ. Just as the church is the body of which Christ is the head, so husbands and wives together form a single body. The thing of primary importance is not who tells whom what to do, but rather the union, the dynamic interrelation of the two. Only within union does the ordering of life within the family begin to make sense. Then Paul reaches back to creation, paraphrasing Genesis 2:24: "A man shall leave his father and mother and be joined to his wife, and the two shall become one flesh."

Given Paul's schooling in the law of Israel, given the Roman culture of the day, one who reads this passage has to agree that Paul assigns primary leadership in the Christian home to the husband. What other conclusion would we expect him to reach? What is remarkable is the emphasis on mutual dependence, on loving relationship and on Christ-like self-giving. In a harsh culture in which infidelity was the rule for most husbands, here is a picture of Christian marriage of great tenderness and beauty. Instead of belaboring Paul for his chauvinism we ought to congratulate him for the breadth of his vision.

Of all the phrases in this passage, I suppose the one that would be rated most objectionable by contemporary readers would be, "Let wives also be subject in everything to their husbands." I read this verse recently during worship and there was a great stir in the congregation and not a small amount of audible laughter. Talk about a cultural contrast! Modern readers should stay with it here rather than push the text aside with an impatient sigh. Let's listen beneath the words to what is being said by Paul and by the spirit of God through him. A reader needs to feel the pulse of Paul's passion for life lived under the lordship of Jesus Christ, life in one's home as well as elsewhere. What is the rule of life for the Christian? Not independence but interrelatedness. This is where freedom and self-discovery lie. Yes, Paul begins, "Wives, be subject to your husbands." Yes, he says, "The husband is the head of the wife." Yes, he repeats himself, "Let wives also be subject in everything to their husbands." No one could deny that he believes the husband is the head of the house. What is notable is that he hedges this on every side with qualifying statements: "Be subject to your husbands, *as to the Lord*," and he means the Lord Jesus. "For the husband is the head of the wife *as Christ is the head of the church*." And when he has said that wives should be subject to their husbands "in everything," he launches into a sermonette on the imperative of love. Four times he admonishes husbands to love their wives, using words like nourish and cherish. While he says that children should obey their parents and slaves should obey their masters, he does not say that wives should obey their husbands. Markus Barth makes this observation:

> The Bridegroom-Bride relationship between Christ and the church is Paul's substitute for a law, a prescription, a fixed custom of conduct in marriage. The spouses are responsible only to God's Messiah who "loved" them and whom they "fear" (5:25,21), to one another in their unique and ever new bond of fidelity, and to the church's missionary task in its environment.[4]

The husband is not like Christ by being the head of the house, but by self-giving love. Perhaps it is passages like this one that have given us the phrase "holy matrimony." Why "holy"? Holy in the root sense of the word, "set apart for the service of God." Surely this is what Paul teaches here, that the Christian husband and wife, in the very nature of their relationship modeled on that of Christ and the church, are set apart for the service of God. Their own bond of human love is welded together in a mutual love for Christ and commitment to his church. This is the vision for marriage Paul projects, the ideal toward which he points. When Christian marriage partners own this ideal, it gives them grace and strength to work through the inevitable conflicts that arise between them. Because of Christ they commit themselves to what is possible for one another.

The following sections of the text are addressed to the relationship between parents and children and between slaves and masters, who also live under the same roof. Obviously this chapter can only make a few general comments on subjects of such broad dimension. Paul's opening admonition is still in force: "Be subject to one another out of reverence for Christ." This "how to get along at home" section of Ephesians is far more than a vest pocket set of moral rules. All the advice given here bears the stamp of Christ's self-giving love. It permeates Paul's thought and writing, which is therefore full of life. One's sexuality, one's family, one's economic life as reflected in the ownershp of slaves, in fact one's whole social structure is to be marked by one's acceptance into the family of God as a forgiven sinner and an heir to the promises of God. Yes, children are to obey their parents, and slaves are to obey their masters, while parents and slave owners alike owe a profound obedience to the Lord Jesus Christ. Even as Paul issues his imperatives for obedience, he immediately hedges the command on every side with admonitions of Christ-like care on the part of those who exercise authority. The breadth and compassion of Paul breathes in every line of this text.

One note before leaving the passage: Contemporary Christians do not understand Paul's advice to slaves and slave owners to be an affirmation of slavery by scripture. Instead, it is a compassionate concern that Christian conscience be tender in the midst of an institution firmly embedded in Roman culture. The death knell of slavery had already sounded in the gospel's clarion call to freedom in Jesus Christ.

Notes

1. Wayne A. Meeks, p. 106.
2. Ibid., p. 167.
3. Ibid., p. 106.
4. Markus Barth, *Ephesians 4-6*, p. 712.

17. In Spiritual Warfare

6:10-20

The text to be dealt with in this chapter is written as a military metaphor. The Christian life is a battle waged against an adversary of cosmic spiritual power. The struggle would be hopeless were it not for the strength of God available for the believer, who, therefore, must be careful to "put on the whole armor of God." The primary image the metaphor presents here is that of readiness for the conflict, similar to how a soldier would prepare armor and weapons for a battle. Every piece of equipment is of superior quality, splendid in its design and appearance. The command is to stand firm, giving no ground to the enemy, and the mood is that of shining confidence. Though the enemy is clever and comes against God's children with a strength belonging to the Prince of Darkness, yet God's light and truth are stronger still.

For clarity and convenience, then, let me divide the text. Verses 10-12 deal with the Adversary; verses 13-17 with the armor; and verses 18-20 with the attitude.

The Adversary

Paul writes, "For we are not contending against flesh and blood, but . . . against the world rulers of this present darkness, against the spiritual hosts of wickedness in the heavenly places." That's a hair-raising statement. In chapters 5 and 6 of Ephesians, Paul has been giving advice about domestic order and tranquility, about relationships in the home: husbands and wives, parents and children, slaves and masters, all living together in the love of Christ. Then, right in the middle of this rather down-to-earth exhortation, we are suddenly confronted with the dark domain of the devil, "the spiritual hosts of wickedness." Where did that come from? Why inject it here? Perhaps because Paul is summarizing, winding up the letter. In the first three chapters, in a mood of praise and joy, he has been setting forth the mystery of Christ, of God's accepting grace in him through which the whole world can find faith, unity, and meaning. In the last three chapters, he turns to practical application, how to live out the meaning of Jesus from day to day. Looking at the surrounding Roman culture, Paul is impressed with the almost overwhelming strength of evil against which Christians must contend. He sees Mars, the god of war; Venus, the goddess of beauty, love, and fertility; and Bacchus, the god of wild and profligate living. He sees the degeneracy of the empire, the greed of its citizens, the emptiness of meaning that marks it so indelibly, the vacuum of moral value and substance. And so he says, "We wrestle not against flesh and blood" (KJV). Or, as Phillips translates it, "Our fight is not against any physical enemy." There is an adversary who seeks to suck life dry of purpose and beauty, who withers away the soul and steals our birthright as children of God.

Contemporary Christians face a double danger when considering what the Bible says about the nature of evil. The first danger is to embrace everything without thinking. The second danger is to reject everything without thinking. In either case the approach is a shallow one. Danger number one is to start reading the exorcism stories of the Gospels or a text like this one and then to fill the world with demons, seeing Satan present everywhere with emissaries behind every bush. That spills over into craziness. It's also a pretty good dodge for accepting responsibility for our own actions, since we can blame our hostility on a pervasive evil presence.

Those of us who are overly superstitious about the devil ought to take a lesson from Jesus, whose custom was not to preach the threatening rule of Satan but the joyous rule of God. Jesus does not engage in idle speculation about the nature of evil or the person of Satan. When he meets those in bondage to Satan's chaotic rule he uses no secret incantations, no special liturgies, no symbolic actions or magical powders, as did the exorcists of the day. On the contrary, he invariably makes an appeal to faith in God, confronting evil with a level eye and with authoritative love. Jesus demythologizes the demonology of the day.[1]

Danger number two is to read the New Testament material on Satan and then reject it as superstitious nonsense from the first century. This is to accept the notion that truth is born with us and that a scientific age like ours necessarily knows more about the nature of evil than a nonscientific age. That's a big leap of faith. Are we more finely tuned to the mysteries than previous generations? Do we know more than they about ultimate reality? Maybe our absorption with the material world deadens our sensitivity to the spiritual world and to the intuitive side of our nature. Convinced that the visible world is all that is real, we find it easy to dismiss the demonic in our devotion to rationality.

So many people have trouble with the Bible's way of personifying evil as Satan, archenemy of God, that it deserves an inquisitive comment or two. Begin here: We don't have trouble accepting the dark nature of evil in our world. If we were to grow quiet for a moment thinking about it, we would readily agree that the face of evil in our world, its very nature, is terrifying, overwhelming, utterly menacing. Consider the racial genocide in Cambodia after the fall of Saigon. Maybe you saw the horror of it in the movie *The Killing Fields.* Names like Buchenwald and Treblinka still strike our ears with shock and unbelief, as we see staccato images of gas ovens and piles of emaciated bodies. Only the distance of those events from our personal lives hides their stark terror. And what of the hatred and fear between nations that have built weapons capable of destroying every human being on earth and devastating this beautiful planet with its delicate life systems?

The biblical writers do not speak of evil as philosophers might, nor can we. We are involved, we are in the struggle; we are under attack; and the fight is sometimes so real that we can feel the cold breath of the Adversary. Experientially, evil meets us as a presence that is not less than personal but more than personal. That's why the biblical writers speak of the Prince of Darkness, the Deceiver, the Evil One. Listen to Dostoyevsky in *The Idiot,* where Lebedyev says, "For the devil is a mighty menacing spirit, but he has not the horns and hooves you've invented for him."[2] It is difficult to understand human history and its interminable cruelty and war without the category of the demonic. Paul felt it and wrote, "We wrestle not against flesh and blood" (KJV).

The Armor

As Paul writes to the Ephesians, he is wrist-chained to a Roman guard, a legionnaire. Contact that close would make the apostle aware of every detail of the guard's apparel as well as his character and person. Perhaps it was this soldier's equipment that suggested to Paul the nature of the Christian's equipment for spiritual warfare: belt, breastplate, sandals, shield, helmet, and sword. Paul begins by telling his readers to "put on the whole armor of God." This was a language that came readily to Paul's mind for several reasons: He experienced living for Jesus Christ as a battle; he was familiar with Old Testament military images; he saw Roman legions present throughout the empire. And so he wrote: "Put on the armor of light" (Rom. 13:12); "wage the good warfare" (1 Tim. 1:18); "the weapons of our warfare are not worldly but have divine power to destroy strongholds" (2 Cor. 10:4).

One of the chief points Paul makes in this passage is that the Christian should be ready for the battle. When a soldier knew he would fight the next day, he carefully tended all equipment. He was in trouble if his belt broke, dropping his sword and dagger to the ground, so he did necessary repairs. He soaked his leather shield in water to toughen it and to quench any flaming arrows or javelins that might strike it. He sharpened his sword, made the ties of his helmet secure, and kept the rust off his chest armor. Being ready was half the battle.

In the array of equipment Paul mentions, only one weapon is offensive: the sword, which Paul calls "the word of God." The rest are defensive, suggesting that one who is equipped with spiritual strength will be impervious to enemy attack. Since the equipment is God-given, it will do more than ward off the enemy—it will enable the Christian soldier to hold ground given by the grace of God. The mood of the passage, therefore, is anything but embattled and defensive. The weapons are glorious: We bind our clothing around us and our sword to our side with a belt of truth. We wear the body armor of righteousness to protect heart and life. Sandals give us freedom of movement to spread everywhere a gospel of peace. The shield of faith for protection, the helmet of salvation for joy, and the sword of the spirit, God's invincible word, make us "more than conquerors" (Rom. 8:37) in the battle.

But the struggle is difficult and fraught with danger. From the beginning, the Adversary has a foothold on the terrain of the soul, coming to us from the inside. He already has a place within us. Francis Thompson put it into two lines of poetry:

> And all man's Babylons strive but to impart
> The grandeurs of his Babylonian heart.[3]

The point of all this is that evil does not control us against our will. Yes, parental models profoundly affect our attitudes and actions. Yes, early childhood experiences play a powerful part in our development. But there remains a center within the self that is free. We must give our assent to every action we take, whatever pressures form and direct us. We belong to that which is chaotic and anti-God only as we say yes to the dark side of ourselves: our passion for power over others, our insistence on our own way at all costs, our desire to own no loyalty higher than our own good, our acceptance of this world as the only reality.

Make no mistake about it—there is a battle going on, and the human heart is the battleground. Forces within and without would make life a wasteland. Each of us needs to hear the question personally: Where will you invest your heart? Where will you spend your life energy? To whom will you give your allegiance? For what purpose are you living? These are the real questions. How we answer them will determine who we are and what we will become. Every day I see people whose primary questions seem to be: What kind of a car shall I buy next? Where shall I take my vacation this year? How can I strike it rich? What new activity will make my life more exciting? I want to impress upon you that these are secondary questions at best. When they become primary questions, they lead to triviality, and we end up wondering why life feels so one-dimensional that there is no song in the heart.

Implicit in the text is the plea not to coast along on the seductive values of the secular culture, values that so often turn out to be variations on the theme "Get yours now!" "Dig down deeper," Paul would say. "Open your heart to God, the God who is always in the depths of life." Yes, there are many good things in our culture, but the surface glitter and glamor will not satisfy the soul. Keeping clear on who we are as children of God and on what matters most is what spiritual warfare is all about. It is keeping tuned to the voice of God. It means examining cultural values in the light of the gospel. It is readiness to use heart and hand in the service of Jesus Christ. It means a consistent refusal to embrace darkness and a willingness to open inner doors to the liberating light of God's loving purpose.

The Attitude

How does this section on prayer connect to the previous section on spiritual armor? Closely, according to the commentaries. One principle strand of interpretation calls prayer the seventh piece of armor. Another strand sees prayer as the consistent attitude of the Christian in spiritual warfare. As Markus Barth puts it, "The life of the whole church and of each of its members is depicted here as an uninterrupted stance of prayer and total involvement in the spreading of the gospel."[4]

The impact of the Ephesians passage is that of passionate appeal on the part of the apostle. In no sense is the mood nonchalant, a kind of "Oh, by the way, pray!" To call the mood urgent is not an adequate commentary. The reader feels immersed in the appeal to pray: "Pray at all times in the Spirit, with all prayer and supplication. . . . Keep alert with all perseverance, making supplication for all the saints, and also for me." This is of critical importance, not only in resisting evil, but for the unity of the saints and the proclamation of the gospel. There can be no mistaking the utter dependence of the Christian on the strength of God to live in the world, and there can be no mistaking the utter dependence of the church on its Lord. Only as the church draws on the strength of God will its mission move forward.

Notes

1. Hans Kung, p. 230f.
2. Fyodor Dostoyevsky, *The Idiot,* Constance Garnett, trans. (New York: The Modern Library, 1935), p. 356.
3. Francis Thompson, "The Heart" in *The Poems of Francis Thompson* (London: Oxford University Press, 1937, reprinted 1960), p. 320.
4. Markus Barth, *Ephesians 4-6,* p. 786.

Conclusion: Hallmarks of Ephesians

There is nothing vague or indistinct about the basic message of the book of Ephesians. Indeed, clarity is a distinguishing hallmark of the letter. Paul presents a clear expression of the self-giving of God in Jesus Christ, a clear statement that love is primary in all our relationships, a clear vision of the unity toward which God calls all people, a clear summons to the individual to surrender heart and will in allegiance to Jesus Christ, a clear promise that it is an eternal kingdom toward which we move, and a clear appeal to discipleship and service. This clarity lends force to the book, for no reader can miss what is present everywhere: that Paul's experience of a living Christ, companion for all his journeys, is the one who gives him clarity in life and word.

A second distinguishing hallmark of Ephesians is joy. While Paul's message is one of urgency and ultimate seriousness, scarcely a paragraph is untouched by the joy that rises up like incense from the page. It is this permeating joy, this deep-running river of wondrous discovery that gives Ephesians "its lift and spirit, its light and intensity," as the introduction states. When exhortations are at an end, when worries for the health and safety of the church are at an end, when theological teaching is at an end, Paul's profound experiential joy in an indwelling Christ remains.

A third distinguishing hallmark of the book is social relevance. For all the visionary nature of Ephesians with Paul's talk of coming ages, the principalities and powers, and a Christ ascending far above all the heavens, still Paul turns again and again to the realities of daily life. How is the new life in Christ to be lived out in a culture absorbed in the sensual worship of the gods and goddesses abounding throughout the empire? What should be the nature of relationships under one's own roof? What attributes of character are to mark the Christian, and how do these compare and contrast with attributes visible in non-Christian neighbors? What resources does God provide for those who want to serve the cause of the gospel? Paul's answers, one should be careful to note, do not deny the present world or seek to escape it while waiting for the world to come. On the contrary, he seeks to equip Ephesian believers for daily life, sending them into the midst of it with clarity and joy. They are, after all, God's "workmanship, created in Christ Jesus for good works" (2:10).

A fourth distinguishing hallmark of Ephesians is the compassion of its author. Though Paul was a Roman citizen born into a cosmopolitan empire that had welded many nations into one by the power of its legions, still he was thoroughly steeped in the life and traditions of Judaism. He says it himself in Galatians: "I advanced in Judaism beyond many of my own age among my people, so extremely zealous was I for the traditions of my fathers" (1:14). One can only imagine the inner struggle, the wrestlings with conscience, the examination of his own roots in Judaism that Paul's work among the Gentiles must have caused him. Most Christians can have little comprehension of the revulsion aroused in a faithful Jew of that day by the worship practices, the dietary habits, and the general conduct of Gentile people. Yet, by the leading of God, Paul finds himself the apostle to the Gentiles. He sees the Gentiles responding to the message of the gospel, comes to know them well, discovers that they have the same hunger for God he knows within himself and that the same Christ he loves and serves comes to them as well. He comes, therefore, to love them deeply, a love one cannot overlook in reading this Ephesian letter. In the theology of the first half of Ephesians, Paul marvels at the grace of God, saying, "You who once were far off have been brought near in the blood of Christ. For he is our peace, who has made us both one" (2:13-14). In the ethical sections of the second half, he exhorts the Ephesians to spiritual maturity: "Speaking the truth in love, we are to grow up in every way into him who is the head, into Christ" (4:15). In chapters five and six, Paul is anxious to help the Ephesians to infuse contemporary institutions of marriage, family, and household with the freshness of the love of Christ. He is a pastor full of tenderness. Even when he rebukes, he is full of compassion, wearing his heart on his sleeve.

Finally, if the reader will forgive me for saying it one more time, Jesus Christ is the luminous center and unfading focus of Ephesians. If there is life this book has breathed out across the centuries, it is the life Christ brings to the human heart and to the world, the life of the Christ whose presence fills this letter the way light fills the world when the sun rises. For love of him, Paul preaches across the world of his day; and for love of him, the church, for all its human weakness, makes its way singing across the centuries.

About the Author

Ron James is the Senior Pastor at First Presbyterian Church of Stamford in Stamford, Connecticut. He has previously published *Creed and Christ*, a devotional study of the Apostle's Creed, and has appeared in *Weavings*.

Dr. James enjoys the outdoors, particularly trout fishing, backpacking, and canoeing. He and his wife, Lois, have four children and four grandchildren.